Century 21 Accounting

Advanced
11e
Working Papers
Chapters 15-24

Claudia Bienias Gilbertson, CPA
Retired
North Hennepin Community College
Brooklyn Park, Minnesota

Mark W. Lehman, CPA, CFE
Associate Professor Emeritus
Richard C. Adkerson School of Accountancy
Mississippi State University
Starkville, Mississippi

Australia • Brazil • Mexico • Singapore • United Kingdom • United States

Century 21 Accounting Advanced
Eleventh Edition
Working Papers, Volume 2

Claudia Bienias Gilbertson,
Mark W. Lehman

SVP, GM Skills & Global Product Management: Jonathan Lau

Product Director: Matthew Seeley

Product Manager: Nicole Robinson

Senior Director, Development: Marah Bellegarde

Product Development Manager: Juliet Steiner

Senior Content Manager: Karen Caldwell

Learning Designer: Jennifer Starr

Product Assistant: Nicholas Scaglione

Vice President, Marketing Services: Jennifer Ann Baker

Director, Product Marketing: Jeremy Walts

Marketing Manager: Abigail Hess

Managing Art Director: Jack Pendleton

Digital Delivery Lead: Jim Gilbert

Senior Digital Content Specialist: Jaclyn Hermesmyer

Cover image(s): Shutterstock.com

Production Management and Composition: SPi Global

© 2020, 2015 Cengage Learning, Inc.

ALL RIGHTS RESERVED. No part of this work covered by the copyright herein may be reproduced or distributed in any form or by any means, except as permitted by U.S. copyright law, without the prior written permission of the copyright owner.

For product information and technology assistance, contact us at
Cengage Customer & Sales Support, 1-800-354-9706.

For permission to use material from this text or product,
submit all requests online at **www.cengage.com/permissions.**
Further permissions questions can be e-mailed to
permissionrequest@cengage.com.

Library of Congress Control Number: 2019933620

Student Edition ISBN-13: 978-1-337-79971-3

Cengage
20 Channel Center Street
Boston, MA 02210
USA

Cengage is a leading provider of customized learning solutions with employees residing in nearly 40 different countries and sales in more than 125 countries around the world. Find your local representative at: **www.cengage.com**.

Cengage products are represented in Canada by Nelson Education, Ltd.

To learn more about Cengage platforms and services, register or access your online learning solution, or purchase materials for your course, visit **ngl.cengage.com**.

Notice to the Reader

Publisher does not warrant or guarantee any of the products described herein or perform any independent analysis in connection with any of the product information contained herein. Publisher does not assume, and expressly disclaims, any obligation to obtain and include information other than that provided to it by the manufacturer. The reader is expressly warned to consider and adopt all safety precautions that might be indicated by the activities described herein and to avoid all potential hazards. By following the instructions contained herein, the reader willingly assumes all risks in connection with such instructions. The publisher makes no representations or warranties of any kind, including but not limited to, the warranties of fitness for particular purpose or merchantability, nor are any such representations implied with respect to the material set forth herein, and the publisher takes no responsibility with respect to such material. The publisher shall not be liable for any special, consequential, or exemplary damages resulting, in whole or part, from the readers' use of, or reliance upon, this material.

Printed in the United States of America
Print Number: 03 Print Year: 2020

TO THE STUDENT

These *Working Papers* are to be used in the study of Chapters 15–24 of CENTURY 21 ACCOUNTING ADVANCED, 11E. Forms are provided for:

1. Study Guides
2. Work Together Exercises
3. On Your Own Exercises
4. Application Problems
5. Mastery Problems
6. Challenge Problems
7. Source Documents Problems
8. Reinforcement Activity 4

Printed on each page is the number of the problem in the textbook for which the form is to be used. Also shown is a specific instruction number for which the form is to be used.

You may not be required to use every form that is provided. Your teacher will tell you whether to retain or dispose of the unused pages.

The pages are perforated so they may be removed as the work required in each assignment is completed. The pages will be more easily detached if you crease the sheet along the line of perforations and then remove the sheet by pulling sideways rather than upward.

TABLE OF CONTENTS

Working Papers for Chapter 15
Budgetary Planning and Control • 503

Working Papers for Chapter 16
Management Decision Making Using Cost-Volume-Profit Analysis • 531

Working Papers for Chapter 17
Job Order Costing • 553

Working Papers for Chapter 18
Management Decision Making Using Differential Analysis • 581

Working Papers for Chapter 19
Process Costing, Activity-Based Costing, and Product Pricing • 601

Working Papers for Chapter 20
Internal Control • 647

Working Papers for Chapter 21
Organizational Structure of a Partnership • 671

Working Papers for Chapter 22
Financial Reporting for a Partnership • 693

Working Papers for Chapter 23
Budgeting and Accounting for a Not-for-Profit Organization • 727

Working Papers for Chapter 24
Financial Reporting for a Not-for-Profit Organization • 743

Name	Perfect Score	Your Score
Identifying Accounting Terms	14 Pts.	
Analyzing Procedures for Budgetary Planning and Control	10 Pts.	
Analyzing Accounting Principles for Budgetary Planning and Control	20 Pts.	
Total	44 Pts.	

Part One—Identifying Accounting Terms

Directions: Select the one term in Column I that best fits each definition in Column II. Print the letter identifying your choice in the Answers column.

Column I

A. administrative expenses budget
B. balanced scorecard
C. budget
D. budget period
E. budgeted income statement
F. budgeting
G. cash budget
H. cash payments budget
I. cash receipts budget
J. other revenue and expenses budget
K. performance report
L. purchases budget
M. sales budget
N. selling expenses budget

Column II	***Answers***
1. Planning the financial operations of a business. (p. 432)	**1.** ________
2. A financial road map used by individuals and companies as a guide for spending and saving. (p. 432)	**2.** ________
3. The length of time covered by a budget. (p. 433)	**3.** ________
4. A statement that shows the projected net sales for a budget period. (p. 436)	**4.** ________
5. A statement prepared to show the projected amount of purchases that will be required during a budget period. (p. 437)	**5.** ________
6. A statement prepared to show projected expenditures related directly to the selling operations. (p. 439)	**6.** ________
7. A statement that shows the projected expenses for all operating expenses not directly related to selling operations. (p. 441)	**7.** ________
8. A statement that shows budgeted revenue and expenses from activities other than normal operations. (p. 442)	**8.** ________
9. A statement that shows a company's projected sales, costs, expenses, and net income. (p. 443)	**9.** ________
10. A statement on which projected cash receipts for a budget period are reported. (p. 447)	**10.** ________
11. A statement on which projected cash payments for a budget period are reported. (p. 449)	**11.** ________
12. A statement that shows for each month or quarter a projection of a company's beginning cash balance, cash receipts, cash payments, and ending cash balance. (p. 450)	**12.** ________
13. A report showing a comparison of projected and actual amounts for a specific period. (p. 453)	**13.** ________
14. A planning and measurement system developed by R. S. Kaplan and D. P. Norton to use multiple performance measures to ensure that a company's vision and strategy are reflected in its goals and activities. (p. 453)	**14.** ________

© 2020 Cengage®. May not be scanned, copied or duplicated, or posted to a publicly accessible website, in whole or in part.

Part Two—Analyzing Procedures for Budgetary Planning and Control

Directions: For each of the following items, select the choice that best completes the statement. Print the letter identifying your choice in the Answers column.

Answers

1. Budget preparation begins with (A) projecting selling expenses, (B) preparing an income statement for the current year, (C) identifying company goals, (D) preparing a cash budget. (p. 432) **1.** ______
2. The cash budget is used to (A) manage cash (B) estimate cash shortages and overages, (C) both A and B are correct, (D) none of these. (p. 432) **2.** ______
3. Usually, the budget period is (A) five years, (B) one year, (C) one quarter, (D) one month. (p. 433) **3.** ______
4. The first budget that is usually prepared is the (A) cash payments schedule, (B) cash budget, (C) purchases budget, (D) sales budget. (p. 436) **4.** ______
5. Typical items in the other revenue and expenses budget include all of the following except (A) depreciation expense, (B) gains or losses on the sale of plant assets, (C) interest expense, (D) interest income. (p. 442) **5.** ______
6. Of the following, the only item included in a cash payments budget is (A) buying equipment, (B) sales, (C) depreciation expense on delivery equipment, (D) issuance of note payable. (p. 449) **6.** ______
7. If the actual cash balance is less than the projected balance (A) the reasons for the decrease are determined, (B) action is taken to correct the problem, (C) both A and B, (D) none of these. (p. 450) **7.** ______
8. The reason the actual cash balance may be less than the projected balance is (A) customers are not paying their accounts when they should, (B) expenses are less than budget projections, (C) both A and B, (D) none of the above. (p. 450) **8.** ______
9. On a performance report, an analysis is made of (A) all differences, (B) all positive differences, (C) all negative differences, (D) all significant differences. (p. 453) **9.** ______
10. On a balanced scorecard, the goal of training 50% of employees on more than one task would fall into the (A) learning and growth area, (B) internal business area, (C) customer service area, (D) financial area. (p. 453) **10.** ______

© 2020 Cengage®. May not be scanned, copied or duplicated, or posted to a publicly accessible website, in whole or in part.

Name ______ Date ______ Class ______

Part Three—Analyzing Accounting Principles for Budgetary Planning and Control

Directions: Place a *T* for True or *F* for False in the Answers column to show whether each of the following statements is true or false.

	Answers
1. Two budgets commonly prepared in businesses are the budgeted income statement and the cash budget. (p. 432)	**1.** ______
2. An annual budget is usually divided into weekly budgets. (p. 433)	**2.** ______
3. General economic information is usually not considered when developing a budget. (p. 433)	**3.** ______
4. Since some information will be in conflict with other information, budget decisions are based finally on company records. (p. 433)	**4.** ______
5. A comparative income statement shows items that may be increasing or decreasing at a higher rate than other items on the statement. (p. 434)	**5.** ______
6. Operational plans and goals generally are determined by the company's executive officers and department managers. (p. 435)	**6.** ______
7. The projected amount of future sales determines to some extent the amount that a business can spend for future salaries. (p. 436)	**7.** ______
8. The purchases budget is prepared before the sales budget is approved. (p. 437)	**8.** ______
9. Unit cost is not needed to prepare a purchases budget. (p. 437)	**9.** ______
10. The amount of projected uncollectible accounts expense is listed on the administrative expenses budget. (p. 441)	**10.** ______
11. In planning a cash receipts budget, consideration is given to projected purchases of equipment and other assets. (p. 447)	**11.** ______
12. In planning a cash receipts budget, consideration is given to the effect of projected cash sales. (p. 447)	**12.** ______
13. In planning a cash payments budget, consideration is given to expected receipts from customers on account. (p. 449)	**13.** ______
14. The amount of payroll taxes expense paid is listed separately on the cash payments budget. (p. 449)	**14.** ______
15. The amount of projected depreciation expense is listed on the cash payments schedule. (p. 449)	**15.** ______
16. A cash budget is prepared from the information contained in the cash receipts budget and the cash payments budget. (p. 450)	**16.** ______
17. The first quarter beginning cash balance of a cash budget is taken from the balance sheet of the previous fiscal year. (p. 450)	**17.** ______
18. A performance report compares actual amounts with projected amounts for the same period, whereas a comparative income statement compares actual amounts of one period with actual amounts of a prior period. (p. 453)	**18.** ______
19. The balanced scorecard develops performance measures in four areas. (p. 453)	**19.** ______
20. The balanced scorecard system emphasizes that there is a cause-and-effect relationship between the four focus areas. (p. 454)	**20.** ______

© 2020 Cengage®. May not be scanned, copied or duplicated, or posted to a publicly accessible website, in whole or in part.

Name ______________________ Date ____________ Class ____________

15-1 WORK TOGETHER (LO2, 3), p. 438

Preparing a sales budget and a purchases budget

1.

Maddox Corporation
Sales Budget
For Year Ended December 31, 20X3 — Schedule 1

	Annual Budget	Quarter			
		1st	2nd	3rd	4th
Actual Unit Sales, 20X2	90,000	17,000	19,000	24,000	30,000
Sales Percentage by Quarter					
Projected Unit Sales, 20X3	100,000				
Times Unit Sales Price					
Net Sales					

2.

Maddox Corporation
Purchases Budget
For Year Ended December 31, 20X3 — Schedule 2

	Quarter			
	1st	2nd	3rd	4th
Unit Sales for Quarter	18,900			
Ending Inventory	4,200			
Total Units Needed	23,100			
Less Beginning Inventory	3,800			
Purchases	19,300			
Times Unit Cost	$7.00			
Cost of Purchases	$135,100			

© 2020 Cengage®. May not be scanned, copied or duplicated, or posted to a publicly accessible website, in whole or in part.

15-1 ON YOUR OWN (LO2, 3), p. 438

Preparing a sales budget and a purchases budget

1.

Northstar, Inc. Sales Budget For Year Ended December 31, 20X3					Schedule 1
	Annual Budget	**Quarter**			
		1st	**2nd**	**3rd**	**4th**
Actual Unit Sales, 20X2	200,000	40,000	48,000	52,000	60,000
Sales Percentage by Quarter					
Projected Unit Sales, 20X3	220,000				
Times Unit Sales Price					
Net Sales					

2.

Northstar, Inc. Purchases Budget For Year Ended December 31, 20X3				Schedule 2
	Quarter			
	1st	**2nd**	**3rd**	**4th**
Unit Sales for Quarter		52,800		
Ending Inventory		14,300		
Total Units Needed		67,100		
Less Beginning Inventory		13,200		
Purchases		53,900		
Times Unit Cost		$3.50		
Cost of Purchases		$188,650		

© 2020 Cengage®. May not be scanned, copied or duplicated, or posted to a publicly accessible website, in whole or in part.

Name ______________________ Date ____________ Class ____________

15-2 WORK TOGETHER (LO4, 5, 6, 7), p. 445

Preparing budgets for selling expenses, administrative expenses, and other expenses and preparing a budgeted income statement.

1.

Maddox Corporation
Selling Expenses Budget
For Year Ended December 31, 20X3 — Schedule 3

	Annual Budget	Quarter			
		1st	2nd	3rd	4th
Advertising Expense		$ 7,090		$10,010	
Delivery Expense		14,180		20,030	
Depr. Expense—Delivery Equipment		2,000		2,000	
Depr. Expense—Warehouse Equipment		1,250		1,250	
Miscellaneous Expense—Sales		11,340		16,020	
Salary Expense—Sales		17,010		24,030	
Supplies Expense—Sales		5,670		8,010	
Total Selling Expenses		$58,540		$81,350	

2.

Maddox Corporation
Administrative Expenses Budget
For Year Ended December 31, 20X3 — Schedule 4

	Annual Budget	Quarter			
		1st	2nd	3rd	4th
Depr. Expense—Office Equipment		$ 1,000		$ 1,000	
Insurance Expense		1,500		1,500	
Miscellaneous Expense—Admin.		750		750	
Payroll Taxes Expense		2,640		3,480	
Rent Expense		6,000		6,000	
Salary Expense—Administrative		5,000		5,000	
Supplies Expense—Administrative		2,000		2,000	
Uncollectible Accounts Expense		1,420		2,000	
Utilities Expense		7,090		10,010	
Total Administrative Expenses		$27,400		$31,740	

© 2020 Cengage®. May not be scanned, copied or duplicated, or posted to a publicly accessible website, in whole or in part.

3.

Maddox Corporation Other Revenue and Expenses Budget For Year Ended December 31, 20X3					Schedule 5
	Annual Budget	Quarter			
		1st	2nd	3rd	4th
Other Expenses:					
Interest Expense					

4.

Maddox Corporation Budgeted Income Statement For Year Ended December 31, 20X3					Schedule 6
	Annual Budget	Quarter			
		1st	2nd	3rd	4th
Operating Revenue:					
Net Sales (Schedule 1)		$283,500		$400,500	
Cost of Merchandise Sold:					
Beginning Inventory		$ 26,600		$ 37,100	
Purchases (Schedule 2)		135,100		196,700	
Total Merchandise Available		$161,700		$233,800	
Less Ending Inventory		29,400		46,900	
Cost of Merchandise Sold		$132,300		$186,900	
Gross Profit on Sales		$151,200		$213,600	
Operating Expenses:					
Selling Expenses (Schedule 3)		$ 58,540		$ 81,350	
Admin. Expenses (Schedule 4)		27,400		31,740	
Total Operating Expenses		$ 85,940		$113,090	
Income from Operations		$ 65,260		$100,510	
Other Expenses (Schedule 5)		630		630	
Net Income before Federal Income Tax		$ 64,630		$ 99,880	
Federal Income Tax Expense		13,570		20,970	
Net Income after Federal Income Tax		$ 51,060		$ 78,910	

© 2020 Cengage®. May not be scanned, copied or duplicated, or posted to a publicly accessible website, in whole or in part.

Name ______________________ Date ____________ Class ____________

15-2 ON YOUR OWN (LO4, 5, 6, 7), p. 446

Preparing budgets for selling expenses, administrative expenses, and other expenses and preparing a budgeted income statement

1.

Northstar, Inc.
Selling Expenses Budget
For Year Ended December 31, 20X3 — Schedule 3

	Annual Budget	Quarter			
		1st	2nd	3rd	4th
Advertising Expense			$ 17,420		$ 21,780
Delivery Expense			28,310		35,390
Depr. Expense—Delivery Equipment			2,500		2,500
Depr. Expense—Warehouse Equipment			5,000		5,000
Miscellaneous Expense—Sales			21,780		27,230
Salary Expense—Sales			30,490		38,120
Supplies Expense—Sales			8,710		10,890
Total Selling Expenses			$114,210		$140,910

2.

Northstar, Inc.
Administrative Expenses Budget
For Year Ended December 31, 20X3 — Schedule 4

	Annual Budget	Quarter			
		1st	2nd	3rd	4th
Depr. Expense—Office Equipment			$ 3,750		$ 3,750
Insurance Expense			3,000		3,000
Miscellaneous Expense—Admin.			2,000		2,000
Payroll Taxes Expense			4,710		5,620
Rent Expense			6,000		6,000
Salary Expense—Administrative			8,750		8,750
Supplies Expense—Administrative			3,600		3,600
Uncollectible Accounts Expense			1,740		2,180
Utilities Expense			26,140		32,670
Total Administrative Expenses			$59,690		$67,570

© 2020 Cengage®. May not be scanned, copied or duplicated, or posted to a publicly accessible website, in whole or in part.

15-2 ON YOUR OWN (concluded)

3.

Northstar, Inc. Other Revenue and Expenses Budget For Year Ended December 31, 20X3					Schedule 5
	Annual Budget	**Quarter**			
		1st	**2nd**	**3rd**	**4th**
Other Expenses:					
Interest Expense					

4.

Northstar, Inc. Budgeted Income Statement For Year Ended December 31, 20X3					Schedule 6
	Annual Budget	**Quarter**			
		1st	**2nd**	**3rd**	**4th**
Operating Revenue:					
Net Sales (Schedule 1)			$435,600		$544,500
Cost of Merchandise Sold:					
Beginning Inventory			$ 46,200		$ 57,750
Purchases (Schedule 2)			188,650		215,250
Total Merchandise Available			$234,850		$273,000
Less Ending Inventory			50,050		42,000
Cost of Merchandise Sold			$184,800		$231,000
Gross Profit on Sales			$250,800		$313,500
Operating Expenses:					
Selling Expenses (Schedule 3)			$114,210		$140,910
Admin. Expenses (Schedule 4)			59,690		67,570
Total Operating Expenses			$173,900		$208,480
Income from Operations			$ 76,900		$105,020
Other Expenses (Schedule 5)			1,000		1,000
Net Income before Federal Income Tax			$ 75,900		$104,020
Federal Income Tax Expense			15,940		21,840
Net Income after Federal Income Tax			$ 59,960		$ 82,180

© 2020 Cengage®. May not be scanned, copied or duplicated, or posted to a publicly accessible website, in whole or in part.

Name ______________________ Date ____________ Class ____________

15-3 WORK TOGETHER (LO8, 9, 10), p. 451

Preparing a cash receipts budget, a cash payments budget, and a cash budget

1.

Maddox Corporation
Cash Receipts Budget
For Year Ended December 31, 20X3 — Schedule A

	Quarter			
	1st	2nd	3rd	4th
Cash Receipts from Sales:				
Prior Year's 4th-Quarter Sales				
1st-Quarter Sales		$ 97,810		
2nd-Quarter Sales		205,730		
3rd-Quarter Sales				
4th-Quarter Sales				
Total Cash Receipts from Sales		$303,540		
Cash Receipts from Other Sources:				
Note Payable to Bank				
Total Cash Receipts		$303,540		

© 2020 Cengage®. May not be scanned, copied or duplicated, or posted to a publicly accessible website, in whole or in part.

15-3 WORK TOGETHER (concluded)

2.

Maddox Corporation Cash Payments Budget For Year Ended December 31, 20X3				Schedule B
	Quarter			
	1st	2nd	3rd	4th
From Purchases:				
Prior Year's 4th Quarter				
1st-Quarter Purchases		$ 54,040		
2nd-Quarter Purchases		93,240		
3rd-Quarter Purchases				
4th-Quarter Purchases				
Total Payments from Purchases		$147,280		
For Operating Expenses:				
Cash Selling Expenses		$ 61,720		
Cash Administrative Expenses		26,040		
Total Cash Operating Expenses		$ 87,760		
Other Cash Payments:				
Federal Income Tax Expense		$ 15,660		
Fixed Asset Purchases				
Cash Dividend		2,500		
Note Payable and Interest				
Total Other Cash Payments		$ 18,160		
Total Cash Payments		$253,200		

3.

Maddox Corporation Cash Budget For Year Ended December 31, 20X3				
	Quarter			
	1st	2nd	3rd	4th
Cash Balance—Beginning	$ 9,500			
Cash Receipts Budget (Schedule A)	354,360			
Cash Available	$363,860			
Less Cash Payments (Schedule B)	299,600			
Cash Balance—Ending	$ 64,260			

© 2020 Cengage®. May not be scanned, copied or duplicated, or posted to a publicly accessible website, in whole or in part.

Name ________________ Date ________ Class ________

15-3 ON YOUR OWN (LO8, 9, 10), p. 451

Preparing a cash receipts budget, a cash payments budget, and a cash budget

1.

Northstar, Inc. Cash Receipts Budget For Year Ended December 31, 20X3 — Schedule A				
	Quarter			
	1st	**2nd**	**3rd**	**4th**
Cash Receipts from Sales:				
Prior Year's 4th-Quarter Sales	$214,080			
1st-Quarter Sales	199,650			
2nd-Quarter Sales			$194,280	
3rd-Quarter Sales			259,550	
4th-Quarter Sales				
Total Cash Receipts from Sales	$413,730		$453,830	
Cash Receipts from Other Sources:				
Note Payable to Bank	30,000			
Total Cash Receipts	$443,730		$453,830	

© 2020 Cengage®. May not be scanned, copied or duplicated, or posted to a publicly accessible website, in whole or in part.

2.

Northstar, Inc.
Cash Payments Budget
For Year Ended December 31, 20X3
Schedule B

	Quarter			
	1st	2nd	3rd	4th
From Purchases:				
Prior Year's 4th Quarter	$ 51,190			
1st-Quarter Purchases	105,110			
2nd-Quarter Purchases			$ 66,030	
3rd-Quarter Purchases			135,140	
4th-Quarter Purchases				
Total Payments from Purchases	$156,300		$201,170	
For Operating Expenses:				
Cash Selling Expenses	$ 88,940		$115,620	
Cash Administrative Expenses	49,230		56,670	
Total Cash Operating Expenses	$138,170		$172,290	
Other Cash Payments:				
Federal Income Tax Expense	$ 12,570		$ 17,910	
Fixed Asset Purchases	100,000			
Cash Dividend	6,000		6,000	
Note Payable and Interest				
Total Other Cash Payments	$118,570		$ 23,910	
Total Cash Payments	$413,040		$397,370	

3.

Northstar, Inc.
Cash Budget
For Year Ended December 31, 20X3

	Quarter			
	1st	2nd	3rd	4th
Cash Balance—Beginning	$ 7,250			
Cash Receipts Budget (Schedule A)	443,730			
Cash Available	$450,980			
Less Cash Payments (Schedule B)	413,040			
Cash Balance—Ending	$ 37,940			

© 2020 Cengage®. May not be scanned, copied or duplicated, or posted to a publicly accessible website, in whole or in part.

Name ______________________ Date ____________ Class ____________

15-4 WORK TOGETHER (LO11), p. 456

Completing a performance report

1., 2.

Maddox Corporation Performance Report For Quarter Ended March 31, 20X3				
	Budget	**Actual**	**Over (Under)**	
			Amount	**Percentage**
Unit Sales	18,900	19,500		
Operating Revenue:				
Net Sales	$283,500	$292,500		
Cost of Merchandise Sold	132,300	137,500		
Gross Profit on Operations	$151,200	$155,000		
Operating Expenses:				
Selling Expenses:				
Advertising Expense	$ 7,090	$ 7,000		
Delivery Expense	14,180	14,900		
Depr. Expense—Delivery Equipment	2,000	2,000		
Depr. Expense—Warehouse Equipment	1,250	1,250		
Miscellaneous Expense—Sales	11,340	11,800		
Salary Expense—Sales	17,010	17,550		
Supplies Expense—Sales	5,670	6,000		
Total Selling Expenses	$ 58,540	$ 60,500		
Administrative Expenses:				
Depr. Expense—Office Equipment	$ 1,000	$ 1,000		
Insurance Expense	1,500	1,500		
Miscellaneous Expense—Administrative	750	710		
Payroll Taxes Expense	2,640	2,710		
Rent Expense	6,000	6,000		
Salary Expense—Administrative	5,000	5,000		
Supplies Expense—Administrative	2,000	2,100		
Uncollectible Accounts Expense	1,420	1,450		
Utilities Expense	7,090	7,100		
Total Administrative Expenses	$ 27,400	$ 27,570		
Total Operating Expenses	$ 85,940	$ 88,070		
Income from Operations	$ 65,260	$ 66,930		
Other Expenses	630	630		
Net Income before Federal Income Tax	$ 64,630	$ 66,300		
Federal Income Tax Expense	13,570	13,923		
Net Income after Federal Income Tax	$ 51,060	$ 52,377		

© 2020 Cengage®. May not be scanned, copied or duplicated, or posted to a publicly accessible website, in whole or in part.

15-4 ON YOUR OWN (LO11), p. 456

Completing a performance report

1., 2.

Northstar, Inc.
Performance Report
For Quarter Ended March 31, 20X3

	Budget	Actual	Over (Under)	
			Amount	Percentage
Unit Sales	44,000	44,100		
Operating Revenue:				
Net Sales	$363,000	$363,830		
Cost of Merchandise Sold	151,250	154,350		
Gross Profit on Operations	$211,750	$209,480		
Operating Expenses:				
Selling Expenses:				
Advertising Expense	$ 14,520	$ 14,000		
Delivery Expense	23,600	23,000		
Depr. Expense—Delivery Equipment	2,500	2,500		
Depr. Expense—Warehouse Equipment	5,000	5,000		
Miscellaneous Expense—Sales	18,150	19,200		
Salary Expense—Sales	25,410	25,500		
Supplies Expense—Sales	7,260	7,500		
Total Selling Expenses	$ 96,440	$ 96,700		
Administrative Expenses:				
Depr. Expense—Office Equipment	$ 3,750	$ 3,750		
Insurance Expense	3,000	3,000		
Miscellaneous Expense—Administrative	2,000	2,010		
Payroll Taxes Expense	4,100	4,050		
Rent Expense	6,000	6,000		
Salary Expense—Administrative	8,750	9,200		
Supplies Expense—Administrative	3,600	3,550		
Uncollectible Accounts Expense	1,450	1,550		
Utilities Expense	21,780	21,500		
Total Administrative Expenses	$ 54,430	$ 54,610		
Total Operating Expenses	$150,870	$151,310		
Income from Operations	$ 60,880	$ 58,170		
Other Expenses	1,000	1,000		
Net Income before Federal Income Tax	$ 59,880	$ 57,170		
Federal Income Tax Expense	12,570	12,006		
Net Income after Federal Income Tax	$ 47,310	$ 45,164		

© 2020 Cengage®. May not be scanned, copied or duplicated, or posted to a publicly accessible website, in whole or in part.

Name ______ Date ______ Class ______

15-1 APPLICATION PROBLEM (LO2, 3), p. 460

Preparing a sales budget and a purchases budget

1.

Craine Corporation
Sales Budget
For Year Ended December 31, 20X3 — Schedule 1

	Annual Budget	Quarter			
		1st	2nd	3rd	4th
Actual Unit Sales, 20X2					
Sales Percentage by Quarter					
Projected Unit Sales, 20X3					
Times Unit Sales Price					
Net Sales					

2.

Craine Corporation
Purchases Budget
For Year Ended December 31, 20X3 — Schedule 2

	Quarter			
	1st	2nd	3rd	4th
Unit Sales for Quarter				
Ending Inventory				
Total Units Needed				
Less Beginning Inventory				
Purchases				
Times Unit Cost				
Cost of Purchases				

© 2020 Cengage®. May not be scanned, copied or duplicated, or posted to a publicly accessible website, in whole or in part.

15-2 APPLICATION PROBLEM (LO4, 5, 6, 7), p. 460

Preparing budgets for selling expenses, administrative expenses, and other expenses and preparing a budgeted income statement

1.

Craine Corporation
Selling Expenses Budget
For Year Ended December 31, 20X3 — Schedule 3

	Annual Budget	Quarter			
		1st	2nd	3rd	4th
Advertising Expense					
Delivery Expense					
Depr. Expense—Delivery Equipment					
Depr. Expense—Warehouse Equipment					
Miscellaneous Expense—Sales					
Salary Expense—Sales					
Supplies Expense—Sales					
Total Selling Expenses					

2.

Craine Corporation
Administrative Expenses Budget
For Year Ended December 31, 20X3 — Schedule 4

	Annual Budget	Quarter			
		1st	2nd	3rd	4th
Depr. Expense—Office Equipment					
Insurance Expense					
Miscellaneous Expense—Admin.					
Payroll Taxes Expense					
Rent Expense					
Salary Expense—Administrative					
Supplies Expense—Administrative					
Uncollectible Accounts Expense					
Utilities Expense					
Total Administrative Expenses					

© 2020 Cengage®. May not be scanned, copied or duplicated, or posted to a publicly accessible website, in whole or in part.

Name ______________________ Date ____________ Class ____________

15-2 APPLICATION PROBLEM (concluded)

3.

Craine Corporation Other Revenue and Expenses Budget For Year Ended December 31, 20X3 — Schedule 5					
	Annual Budget	Quarter			
		1st	2nd	3rd	4th
Other Expenses:					
Interest Expense					

4.

Craine Corporation Budgeted Income Statement For Year Ended December 31, 20X3 — Schedule 6					
	Annual Budget	Quarter			
		1st	2nd	3rd	4th
Operating Revenue:					
Net Sales (Schedule 1)					
Cost of Merchandise Sold:					
Beginning Inventory					
Purchases (Schedule 2)					
Total Merchandise Available					
Less Ending Inventory					
Cost of Merchandise Sold					
Gross Profit on Sales					
Operating Expenses:					
Selling Expenses (Schedule 3)					
Admin. Expenses (Schedule 4)					
Total Operating Expenses					
Income from Operations					
Other Expenses (Schedule 5)					
Net Income before Federal Income Tax					
Federal Income Tax Expense					
Net Income after Federal Income Tax					

© 2020 Cengage®. May not be scanned, copied or duplicated, or posted to a publicly accessible website, in whole or in part.

15-3 APPLICATION PROBLEM (LO8, 9, 10), p. 461

Preparing a cash receipts budget, a cash payments budget, and a cash budget

1.

Craine Corporation
Cash Receipts Budget
For Year Ended December 31, 20X3 — Schedule A

	Quarter			
	1st	**2nd**	**3rd**	**4th**
Cash Receipts from Sales:				
Prior Year's 4th-Quarter Sales				
1st-Quarter Sales				
2nd-Quarter Sales				
3rd-Quarter Sales				
4th-Quarter Sales				
Total Cash Receipts from Sales				
Cash Receipts from Other Sources:				
Note Payable to Bank				
Total Cash Receipts				

© 2020 Cengage®. May not be scanned, copied or duplicated, or posted to a publicly accessible website, in whole or in part.

Name ______________________ Date ____________ Class ____________

15-3 APPLICATION PROBLEM (concluded)

2.

Craine Corporation
Cash Payments Budget
For Year Ended December 31, 20X3

Schedule B

	Quarter			
	1st	2nd	3rd	4th
From Purchases:				
Prior Year's 4th Quarter				
1st-Quarter Purchases				
2nd-Quarter Purchases				
3rd-Quarter Purchases				
4th-Quarter Purchases				
Total Payments from Purchases				
For Operating Expenses:				
Cash Selling Expenses				
Cash Administrative Expenses				
Total Cash Operating Expenses				
Other Cash Payments:				
Federal Income Tax Expense				
Fixed Asset Purchases				
Cash Dividend				
Note Payable and Interest				
Total Other Cash Payments				
Total Cash Payments				

3.

Craine Corporation
Cash Budget
For Year Ended December 31, 20X3

	Quarter			
	1st	2nd	3rd	4th
Cash Balance—Beginning				
Cash Receipts Budget (Schedule A)				
Cash Available				
Less Cash Payments (Schedule B)				
Cash Balance—Ending				

© 2020 Cengage®. May not be scanned, copied or duplicated, or posted to a publicly accessible website, in whole or in part.

15-4 APPLICATION PROBLEM (LO11), p. 462

Completing a performance report

1., 2.

Craine Corporation
Performance Report
For Quarter Ended March 31, 20X3

	Budget	Actual	Over (Under)	
			Amount	Percentage
Unit Sales	125,000	127,500		
Operating Revenue:				
Net Sales	$1,750,000	$1,785,000		
Cost of Merchandise Sold	910,300	930,000		
Gross Profit on Operations	$ 839,700	$ 855,000		
Operating Expenses:				
Selling Expenses:				
Advertising Expense	$ 78,750	$ 85,000		
Delivery Expense	35,000	36,000		
Depr. Expense—Delivery Equipment	18,750	18,750		
Depr. Expense—Warehouse Equipment	21,000	21,000		
Miscellaneous Expense—Sales	96,250	95,200		
Salary Expense—Sales	122,500	124,950		
Supplies Expense—Sales	70,000	75,000		
Total Selling Expenses	$ 442,250	$ 455,900		
Administrative Expenses:				
Depr. Expense—Office Equipment	$ 11,000	$ 11,000		
Insurance Expense	3,600	3,600		
Miscellaneous Expense—Administrative	4,000	4,100		
Payroll Taxes Expense	16,630	16,900		
Rent Expense	18,000	18,000		
Salary Expense—Administrative	16,100	16,100		
Supplies Expense—Administrative	7,500	7,100		
Uncollectible Accounts Expense	8,750	8,800		
Utilities Expense	140,000	141,500		
Total Administrative Expenses	$ 225,580	$ 227,100		
Total Operating Expenses	$ 667,830	$ 683,000		
Income from Operations	$ 171,870	$ 172,000		
Other Expenses	5,000	5,000		
Net Income before Federal Income Tax	$ 166,870	$ 167,000		
Federal Income Tax Expense	35,040	35,070		
Net Income after Federal Income Tax	$ 131,830	$ 131,930		

© 2020 Cengage®. May not be scanned, copied or duplicated, or posted to a publicly accessible website, in whole or in part.

Name ________________ Date ________ Class ________

15-M MASTERY PROBLEM (LO2, 3, 4, 5, 6, 7, 8, 9, 10), p. 462

Preparing a budgeted income statement and a cash budget with supporting budgets

1.

ZZZ Company
Sales Budget
For Year Ended December 31, 20X3
Schedule 1

	Annual Budget	Quarter			
		1st	2nd	3rd	4th
Actual Unit Sales, 20X2					
Sales Percentage by Quarter					
Projected Unit Sales, 20X3					
Times Unit Sales Price					
Net Sales					

2.

ZZZ Company
Purchases Budget
For Year Ended December 31, 20X3
Schedule 2

	Quarter			
	1st	2nd	3rd	4th
Unit Sales for Quarter				
Ending Inventory				
Total Units Needed				
Less Beginning Inventory				
Purchases				
Times Unit Cost				
Cost of Purchases				

© 2020 Cengage®. May not be scanned, copied or duplicated, or posted to a publicly accessible website, in whole or in part.

15-M MASTERY PROBLEM (continued)

3.

ZZZ Company
Selling Expenses Budget
For Year Ended December 31, 20X3 — Schedule 3

	Annual Budget	Quarter			
		1st	2nd	3rd	4th
Advertising Expense					
Delivery Expense					
Depr. Expense—Delivery Equipment					
Depr. Expense—Warehouse Equipment					
Miscellaneous Expense—Sales					
Salary Expense—Sales					
Supplies Expense—Sales					
Total Selling Expenses					

4.

ZZZ Company
Administrative Expenses Budget
For Year Ended December 31, 20X3 — Schedule 4

	Annual Budget	Quarter			
		1st	2nd	3rd	4th
Depr. Expense—Office Equipment					
Insurance Expense					
Miscellaneous Expense—Admin.					
Payroll Taxes Expense					
Rent Expense					
Salary Expense—Administrative					
Supplies Expense—Administrative					
Uncollectible Accounts Expense					
Utilities Expense					
Total Administrative Expenses					

© 2020 Cengage®. May not be scanned, copied or duplicated, or posted to a publicly accessible website, in whole or in part.

Name ______________________ Date __________ Class __________

15-M MASTERY PROBLEM (continued)

5.

ZZZ Company Other Revenue and Expenses Budget For Year Ended December 31, 20X3					Schedule 5
	Annual Budget	**Quarter**			
		1st	**2nd**	**3rd**	**4th**
Other Expenses:					
Interest Expense					

6.

ZZZ Company Budgeted Income Statement For Year Ended December 31, 20X3					Schedule 6
	Annual Budget	**Quarter**			
		1st	**2nd**	**3rd**	**4th**
Operating Revenue:					
Net Sales (Schedule 1)					
Cost of Merchandise Sold:					
Beginning Inventory					
Purchases (Schedule 2)					
Total Merchandise Available					
Less Ending Inventory					
Cost of Merchandise Sold					
Gross Profit on Sales					
Operating Expenses:					
Selling Expenses (Schedule 3)					
Admin. Expenses (Schedule 4)					
Total Operating Expenses					
Income from Operations					
Other Expenses (Schedule 5)					
Net Income before Federal Income Tax					
Federal Income Tax Expense					
Net Income after Federal Income Tax					

© 2020 Cengage®. May not be scanned, copied or duplicated, or posted to a publicly accessible website, in whole or in part.

7.

ZZZ Company Cash Receipts Budget For Year Ended December 31, 20X3				Schedule A
	Quarter			
	1st	2nd	3rd	4th
Cash Receipts from Sales:				
Prior Year's 4th-Quarter Sales				
1st-Quarter Sales				
2nd-Quarter Sales				
3rd-Quarter Sales				
4th-Quarter Sales				
Total Cash Receipts from Sales				
Cash Receipts from Other Sources:				
Note Payable to Bank				
Total Cash Receipts				

© 2020 Cengage®. May not be scanned, copied or duplicated, or posted to a publicly accessible website, in whole or in part.

Name ______________________ Date ____________ Class ____________

15-M MASTERY PROBLEM (concluded)

8.

ZZZ Company Cash Payments Budget For Year Ended December 31, 20X3 Schedule B				
	Quarter			
	1st	2nd	3rd	4th
From Purchases:				
Prior Year's 4th Quarter				
1st-Quarter Purchases				
2nd-Quarter Purchases				
3rd-Quarter Purchases				
4th-Quarter Purchases				
Total Payments from Purchases				
For Operating Expenses:				
Cash Selling Expenses				
Cash Administrative Expenses				
Total Cash Operating Expenses				
Other Cash Payments:				
Federal Income Tax Expense				
Fixed Asset Purchases				
Cash Dividend				
Note Payable and Interest				
Total Other Cash Payments				
Total Cash Payments				

9.

ZZZ Company Cash Budget For Year Ended December 31, 20X3				
	Quarter			
	1st	2nd	3rd	4th
Cash Balance—Beginning				
Cash Receipts Budget (Schedule A)				
Cash Available				
Less Cash Payments (Schedule B)				
Cash Balance—Ending				

© 2020 Cengage®. May not be scanned, copied or duplicated, or posted to a publicly accessible website, in whole or in part.

15-C CHALLENGE PROBLEM (LO12), p. 464

Balanced scorecard

1., 2.

Performance Measure	Objective	How Measured	Target Goal
Learning/Growth	Increase the number of cross-trained employees	Number of employees able to perform more than one job	25% of employees are cross-trained
Internal Business			
Customer Service			
Financial			

© 2020 Cengage®. May not be scanned, copied or duplicated, or posted to a publicly accessible website, in whole or in part.

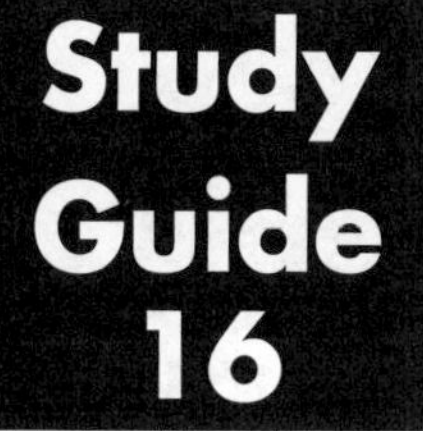

Name	Perfect Score	Your Score
Identifying Accounting Terms	7 Pts.	
Analyzing Accounting Principles for Management Decision Information	13 Pts.	
Examining Procedures for Preparing Management Decision Information	14 Pts.	
Total	34 Pts.	

Part One—Identifying Accounting Terms

Directions: Select the one term in Column I that best fits each definition in Column II. Print the letter identifying your choice in the Answers column.

Column I	Column II	Answers
A. breakeven point	**1.** All costs for a specific period of time. (p. 469)	**1.** ________
B. contribution margin	**2.** An amount spent for one unit of a specific product or service. (p. 469)	**2.** ________
C. fixed costs	**3.** Costs that change in direct proportion to a change in the number of units. (p. 470)	**3.** ________
D. sales mix	**4.** Costs that remain constant regardless of a change in business activity. (p. 470)	**4.** ________
E. total costs	**5.** Income determined by subtracting all variable costs from net sales. (p. 471)	**5.** ________
F. unit cost	**6.** The amount of sales at which net sales is equal to total costs. (p. 474)	**6.** ________
G. variable costs	**7.** The relative distribution of sales among various products. (p. 485)	**7.** ________

© 2020 Cengage®. May not be scanned, copied or duplicated, or posted to a publicly accessible website, in whole or in part.

Part Two—Analyzing Accounting Principles for Management Decision Information

Directions: Place a *T* for True or *F* for False in the Answers column to show whether each of the following statements is true or false.

	Answers
1. If one unit of a product costs \$5.00 and ten units of that product cost \$50.00, the cost is a variable cost. (p. 470)	1. ______
2. Variable costs plotted on a graph become a straight line parallel with the base of the graph. (p. 470)	2. ______
3. Fixed costs plotted on a graph become a straight line parallel with the base of the graph. (p. 470)	3. ______
4. Total variable costs increase as sales increase. (p. 470)	4. ______
5. Total fixed costs increase as sales increase. (p. 470)	5. ______
6. Net sales less selling and administrative expenses equals marginal income. (p. 471)	6. ______
7. Net sales less fixed costs equals contribution margin. (p. 471)	7. ______
8. The point at which no net income is earned and no net loss is incurred is called the gross profit point. (p. 474)	8. ______
9. CVP analysis can be used to calculate the dollar and unit sales needed to earn a specified amount of a planned net income. (p. 479)	9. ______
10. Changes in sales volume will not affect net income. (p. 480)	10. ______
11. The sales line plotted on a graph, starting at zero, represents the unit sales price times the number of units sold. (p. 481)	11. ______
12. At the breakeven point on a graph, the sales and total cost lines intersect. (p. 481)	12. ______
13. If the sales volume is below the breakeven point, the result is a net loss. (p. 481)	13. ______

© 2020 Cengage®. May not be scanned, copied or duplicated, or posted to a publicly accessible website, in whole or in part.

Name ________________________ Date ____________ Class ____________

Part Three—Examining Procedures for Preparing Management Decision Information

Directions: For each item below, select the choice that best completes the sentence. Print the choice in the Answers column.

Answers

1. Unit costs are calculated by (A) dividing total costs by the number of units, (B) multiplying total costs by the number of units, (C) dividing unit costs by the variable costs, (D) multiplying unit costs by the variable costs. (p. 469) **1.** ______

2. When sales increase, a cost that always increases in the same direct proportion is a(n) (A) fixed cost, (B) variable cost, (C) selling expense, (D) administrative expense. (p. 470) **2.** ______

3. The $40.00 paid by a commercial painter for each gallon of paint is a (A) breakeven cost, (B) fixed cost, (C) total cost, (D) variable cost. (p. 470) **3.** ______

4. The $1,200.00 per month rent paid by a physician is a (A) breakeven cost, (B) fixed cost, (C) total cost, (A) variable cost. (p. 470) **4.** ______

5. Gross profit is determined by (A) subtracting the cost of merchandise sold from net sales, (B) subtracting variable costs from net sales, (C) adding net income to administrative expenses, (D) subtracting net income from net sales. (p. 471) **5.** ______

6. Contribution margin is determined by (A) subtracting the cost of merchandise sold from net sales, (B) subtracting variable costs from net sales, (C) adding net income to administrative expenses, (D) subtracting net income from net sales. (p. 471) **6.** ______

7. A company's contribution margin is $200,000.00. It sold 10,000 units. The contribution margin per unit is (A) $0.05, (B) $2.00, (C) $5.00, (D) $20.00. (p. 472) **7.** ______

8. A company's contribution margin is $200,000.00. Net sales equal $500,000.00. The contribution rate is (A) 2.5%, (B) 25%, (C) 40%, (D) 50%. (p. 472) **8.** ______

9. The calculation for the contribution margin rate is (A) contribution margin minus net sales, (B) contribution margin times net sales, (C) contribution margin divided by net sales, (D) contribution margin plus net sales. (p. 472) **9.** ______

10. The breakeven point can be stated in (A) sales dollars, (B) unit sales, (C) both A and B, (D) none of these. (p. 474) **10.** ______

11. A company is considering selling a new product at $100.00 per unit. Variable costs are $25.00 per unit and fixed costs are $75,000.00 per month. The breakeven point in units of this new product is (A) 3,000, (B) 1,000, (C) 750, (D) 600. (p. 477) **11.** ______

12. To earn a net income of $2,000.00, a business with a unit sales price of $24.00, a unit variable cost of $16.00, and total fixed costs of $10,000.00 would need sales of (A) $24,000.00, (B) $30,000.00, (C) $36,000.00, (D) $48,000.00. (p. 479) **12.** ______

13. A change in its production process would allow a business to increase its contribution margin per unit from $10.00 to $12.00, but would increase total fixed costs from $4,000.00 to $5,400.00. The company should change its production process if unit sales are (A) greater than 450 units, (B) greater than 400 units, (C) less than 450 units, (D) less than 400 units. (p. 482) **13.** ______

14. Last year a company sold $150,000.00 of shampoo and $50,000.00 of conditioner. The sales mix for shampoo is (A) 75%, (B) 66%, (C) 33%, (D) 25%. (p. 484) **14.** ______

© 2020 Cengage®. May not be scanned, copied or duplicated, or posted to a publicly accessible website, in whole or in part.

Name ______________________ Date ____________ Class ____________

16-1 WORK TOGETHER (LO1, 2, 3, 4), p. 473

Preparing an income statement with contribution margin

1.

2.

3.

© 2020 Cengage®. May not be scanned, copied or duplicated, or posted to a publicly accessible website, in whole or in part.

16-1 ON YOUR OWN (LO1, 2, 3, 4), p. 473

Preparing an income statement with contribution margin

1.

2.

3.

© 2020 Cengage®. May not be scanned, copied or duplicated, or posted to a publicly accessible website, in whole or in part.

Name ____________ Date ____________ Class ____________

16-2 WORK TOGETHER (LO5, 6), p. 478

Calculating breakeven in sales dollars and unit sales and preparing a breakeven income statement

Cathy's Cakes

Income Statement

For Month Ended July 31, 20--

Operating Revenue:		
Net Sales (7,500 @ $16.00)		120 0 0 0 00
Variable Costs:		
Cost of Merchandise Sold (7,500 @ $9.00)	67 5 0 0 00	
Sales Commissions (7,500 @ $0.40)	3 0 0 0 00	
Delivery Expense (7,500 @ $0.75)	5 6 2 5 00	
Other Variable Selling Costs (7,500 @ $1.65)	12 3 7 5 00	
Other Variable Administrative Costs (7,500 @ $1.00)	7 5 0 0 00	
Total Variable Costs		96 0 0 0 00
Contribution Margin		24 0 0 0 00
Fixed Costs:		
Rent Expense	3 0 0 0 00	
Insurance Expense	1 0 0 0 00	
Other Fixed Selling Costs	7 0 0 0 00	
Other Fixed Administrative Costs	5 0 0 0 00	
Total Fixed Costs		16 0 0 0 00
Net Income		8 0 0 0 00

1. **Breakeven point in sales dollars for July:**

Contribution Margin	÷	**Net Sales**	=	**Contribution Margin Rate**
Total Fixed Costs	÷	**Contribution Margin Rate**	=	**Sales Dollar Breakeven Point**

Unit sales breakeven point for July:

Sales Dollar Breakeven Point	÷	**Unit Sales Price**	=	**Unit Sales Breakeven Point**

© 2020 Cengage®. May not be scanned, copied or duplicated, or posted to a publicly accessible website, in whole or in part.

16-2 WORK TOGETHER (concluded)

2.

© 2020 Cengage®. May not be scanned, copied or duplicated, or posted to a publicly accessible website, in whole or in part.

Name ______________________ Date ____________ Class ____________

16-2 ON YOUR OWN (LO5, 6), p. 478

Calculating breakeven in sales dollars and unit sales and preparing a breakeven income statement

Cathy's Cakes

Income Statement

For Month Ended August 31, 20--

Operating Revenue:		
Net Sales (10,000 @ $16.00)		160,000.00
Variable Costs:		
Cost of Merchandise Sold (10,000 @ $9.85)	98,500.00	
Sales Commissions (10,000 @ $0.45)	4,500.00	
Delivery Expense (10,000 @ $0.80)	8,000.00	
Other Variable Selling Costs (10,000 @ $1.75)	17,500.00	
Other Variable Administrative Costs (10,000 @ $1.15)	11,500.00	
Total Variable Costs		140,000.00
Contribution Margin		20,000.00
Fixed Costs:		
Rent Expense	3,000.00	
Insurance Expense	1,000.00	
Other Fixed Selling Costs	7,000.00	
Other Fixed Administrative Costs	5,000.00	
Total Fixed Costs		16,000.00
Net Income		4,000.00

1. Breakeven point in sales dollars for August:

Contribution Margin	÷	Net Sales	=	Contribution Margin Rate

Total Fixed Costs	÷	Contribution Margin Rate	=	Sales Dollar Breakeven Point

Unit sales breakeven point for August:

Sales Dollar Breakeven Point	÷	Unit Sales Price	=	Unit Sales Breakeven Point

© 2020 Cengage®. May not be scanned, copied or duplicated, or posted to a publicly accessible website, in whole or in part.

16-2 ON YOUR OWN (concluded)

2.

© 2020 Cengage®. May not be scanned, copied or duplicated, or posted to a publicly accessible website, in whole or in part.

Name ______________________ Date ____________ Class ____________

16-3 WORK TOGETHER (LO7, 8, 9), p. 486

Calculating sales to earn a planned net income, the effect of volume and sales price changes, and sales mix

1.

2.

	Per Unit	Number of Units		
		4,000	5,000	6,000

3.

	Current Price			Price Reduction and Sales Volume Increase		
	Per Unit	Units Sold	Total	Per Unit	Units Sold	Total

© 2020 Cengage®. May not be scanned, copied or duplicated, or posted to a publicly accessible website, in whole or in part.

16-3 WORK TOGETHER (concluded)

4. **Product Sales Dollars**

Product Unit Sales

© 2020 Cengage®. May not be scanned, copied or duplicated, or posted to a publicly accessible website, in whole or in part.

Name ______________________ Date ____________ Class ____________

16-3 ON YOUR OWN (LO7, 8, 9), p. 486

Calculating sales to earn a planned net income, the effect of volume and price changes, and sales mix

1.

2.

	Per Unit	Number of Units		
		7,000	8,000	9,000

3.

	Current Price			Price Increase and Sales Volume Decrease		
	Per Unit	Units Sold	Total	Per Unit	Units Sold	Total

© 2020 Cengage®. May not be scanned, copied or duplicated, or posted to a publicly accessible website, in whole or in part.

16-3 ON YOUR OWN (concluded)

4. Product Sales Dollars

Product Unit Sales

© 2020 Cengage®. May not be scanned, copied or duplicated, or posted to a publicly accessible website, in whole or in part.

Name ______________________ Date ______________ Class ______________

16-1 APPLICATION PROBLEM (LO1, 2, 3, 4), p. 488

Preparing an income statement with contribution margin

1.

2.

3.

© 2020 Cengage®. May not be scanned, copied or duplicated, or posted to a publicly accessible website, in whole or in part.

16-2 APPLICATION PROBLEM (LO5, 6), p. 488

Calculating breakeven in sales dollars and unit sales and preparing a breakeven income statement

Bountiful Boards, Inc.

Income Statement

For Month Ended September 30, 20--

Operating Revenue:		
Net Sales (4,000 @ $100.00)		400,000.00
Variable Costs:		
Cost of Merchandise Sold (4,000 @ $30.00)	120,000.00	
Sales Commissions (4,000 @ $2.00)	8,000.00	
Delivery Expense (4,000 @ $1.00)	4,000.00	
Other Variable Selling Costs (4,000 @ $3.00)	12,000.00	
Other Variable Administrative Costs (4,000 @ $4.00)	16,000.00	
Total Variable Costs		160,000.00
Contribution Margin		240,000.00
Fixed Costs:		
Rent Expense	1,000.00	
Insurance Expense	500.00	
Other Fixed Selling Costs	2,000.00	
Other Fixed Administrative Costs	2,500.00	
Total Fixed Costs		6,000.00
Net Income		234,000.00

1. Breakeven point in sales dollars for September:

Unit sales breakeven point for September:

© 2020 Cengage®. May not be scanned, copied or duplicated, or posted to a publicly accessible website, in whole or in part.

Name ______________________ Date ____________ Class ____________

16-2 APPLICATION PROBLEM (concluded)

2.

© 2020 Cengage®. May not be scanned, copied or duplicated, or posted to a publicly accessible website, in whole or in part.

16-3 APPLICATION PROBLEM (LO7, 8, 9), p. 489

Calculating sales, sales mix, and the effect of volume and price changes

1.

2.

	Per Unit	Number of Units		
		4,500	5,500	6,500

3.

	Current Price			Price Reduction and Sales Volume Increase		
	Per Unit	Units Sold	Total	Per Unit	Units Sold	Total

© 2020 Cengage®. May not be scanned, copied or duplicated, or posted to a publicly accessible website, in whole or in part.

Name ______________________ Date ______________ Class ______________

16-3 APPLICATION PROBLEM (concluded)

4. **Product Sales Dollars**

Product Unit Sales

© 2020 Cengage®. May not be scanned, copied or duplicated, or posted to a publicly accessible website, in whole or in part.

16-M MASTERY PROBLEM (LO2, 3, 4, 5, 6, 7), p. 489

Calculating breakeven and the sales required for a desired income

1.

2.

© 2020 Cengage®. May not be scanned, copied or duplicated, or posted to a publicly accessible website, in whole or in part.

Name ______ Date ______ Class ______

16-M MASTERY PROBLEM (concluded)

3. **Breakeven point in sales dollars for April:**

Unit sales breakeven point for April:

4.

© 2020 Cengage®. May not be scanned, copied or duplicated, or posted to a publicly accessible website, in whole or in part.

16-C CHALLENGE PROBLEM (LO3, 9), p. 490

Using contribution margin to analyze sales mix with constraint

1.

2. CM per minute: Model X = ________

CM per minute: Model Y = ________

3.

© 2020 Cengage®. May not be scanned, copied or duplicated, or posted to a publicly accessible website, in whole or in part.

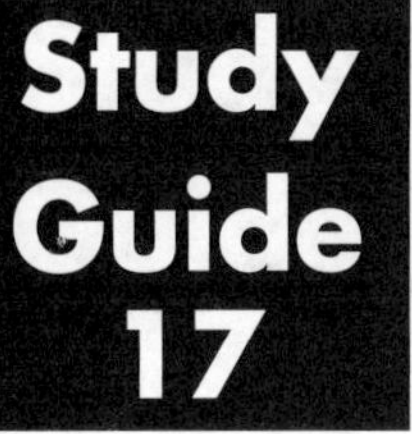

Name	Perfect Score	Your Score
Identifying Accounting Terms	28 Pts.	
Analyzing Manufacturing Cost Accounting Procedures	11 Pts.	
Analyzing the Format of a Statement of Cost of Goods Manufactured	8 Pts.	
Analyzing Transactions for a Manufacturing Business	9 Pts.	
Total	56 Pts.	

Part One—Identifying Accounting Terms

Directions: Select the one term in Column I that best fits each definition in Column II. Print the letter identifying your choice in the Answers column. Note that there are more terms to choose from on the next page.

Column I

A. applied overhead
B. cost ledger
C. direct labor
D. direct materials
E. factory overhead
F. finished goods
G. finished goods ledger
H. indirect labor
I. indirect materials
J. job order costing
K. labor price standard
L. labor price variance
M. labor quantity standard
N. labor quantity variance
O. materials ledger
P. materials price standard
Q. materials price variance
R. materials quantity standard
S. materials quantity variance
T. overapplied overhead
U. process costing
V. standard

Column II	*Answers*
1. Materials that are of significant value in the cost of a finished product and that become an identifiable part of the product. (p. 496)	**1.** ________
2. Salaries of factory workers who make a product. (p. 496)	**2.** ________
3. All expenses other than direct materials and direct labor that apply to making products. (p. 496)	**3.** ________
4. Materials used in the completion of a product that are of insignificant value to justify accounting for separately. (p. 496)	**4.** ________
5. Salaries paid to factory workers who are not actually making products. (p. 496)	**5.** ________
6. Products being manufactured but not yet complete. (p. 496)	**6.** ________
7. Manufactured products that are fully completed. (p. 496)	**7.** ________
8. Measuring the manufacturing costs of a specific order or batch as it goes through the production process (p. 497)	**8.** ________
9. Measuring the manufacturing costs of similar goods as they flow continuously from one production process to another (p. 497)	**9.** ________
10. A ledger containing all records of materials. (p. 497)	**10.** ________
11. A ledger containing all cost sheets for products in the process of being manufactured. (p. 497)	**11.** ________
12. A ledger containing records of all finished goods on hand. (p. 497)	**12.** ________
13. The estimated amount of factory overhead recorded on cost sheets. (p. 507)	**13.** ________
14. The amount by which applied factory overhead is less than actual factory overhead. (p. 510)	**14.** ________
15. The amount by which applied factory overhead is more than actual factory overhead. (p. 510)	**15.** ________

(continued on next page)

© 2020 Cengage®. May not be scanned, copied or duplicated, or posted to a publicly accessible website, in whole or in part.

Column I	Column II	Answers
W. standard costing system	16. A statement showing details about the cost of finished goods. (p. 514)	16. ________
X. statement of cost of goods manufactured	17. An estimated amount of direct materials or direct labor, usually in price or quantity, established for each unit produced. (p. 519)	17. ________
Y. total labor variance		
Z. total materials variance	18. A system of setting standards for each cost of production. (p. 519)	18. ________
AA. underapplied overhead	19. The estimated amount of direct materials to be used per unit of output. (p. 519)	19. ________
AB. work in process	20. The estimated cost per unit of direct materials. (p. 519)	20. ________
	21. The estimated amount of direct labor needed to produce one unit of output. (p. 519)	21. ________
	22. The estimated cost per hour of direct labor. (p. 519)	22. ________
	23. The difference between the actual cost of materials and the expected standard cost of materials. (p. 520)	23. ________
	24. The difference between the actual price paid for materials and the materials price standard at the actual quantity purchased and used. (p. 521)	24. ________
	25. The difference between the actual quantity of materials purchased and used in production and the standard quantity of materials for that level of production at the standard price. (p. 521)	25. ________
	26. The difference between the actual cost of labor and the expected standard cost of labor. (p. 522)	26. ________
	27. The difference between the actual price paid for labor and the labor price standard at the actual quantity used. (p. 523)	27. ________
	28. The difference between the actual quantity of labor used in production and the standard quantity of labor for that level of production at the standard price. (p. 523)	28. ________

© 2020 Cengage®. May not be scanned, copied or duplicated, or posted to a publicly accessible website, in whole or in part.

Name ____________________ Date __________ Class __________

Part Two—Analyzing Manufacturing Cost Accounting Procedures

Directions: Place a *T* for True or *F* for False in the Answers column to show whether each of the following statements is true or false.

	Answers
1. Direct materials and direct labor are included in factory overhead. (p. 496)	1. ______
2. The balance of the general ledger account Materials equals the sum of all the account balances in the materials ledger. (p. 499)	2. ______
3. At the end of each day, job-time records are summarized and direct labor costs are recorded on each job's cost sheet. (p. 504)	3. ______
4. The journal entry for factory payroll includes a debit to factory overhead. (p. 505)	4. ______
5. At the end of a fiscal period, cost sheets for work in process are totaled to determine the ending inventory for the general ledger account Work in Process. (p. 508)	5. ______
6. A debit balance in the factory overhead account indicates that overhead is overapplied. (p. 510)	6. ______
7. The total of all finished goods ledger cards equals the Work in Process inventory account balance. (p. 512)	7. ______
8. Overapplied overhead is listed on an income statement as an addition to the cost of goods sold. (p. 515)	8. ______
9. Once standards are established, they can be compared to actual results to evaluate the efficiency of the manufacturing process. (p. 519)	9. ______
10. A favorable materials price variance cannot have an influence on the materials quantity variance. (p. 521)	10. ______
11. A favorable labor price variance means that the price actually paid for labor was less than the labor price standard. (p. 522)	11. ______

Part Three—Analyzing the Format of a Statement of Cost of Goods Manufactured

Directions: For each numbered line of the Statement of Cost of Goods Manufactured, print in the Answers column the identifying letter of the correct line name. (p. 514)

Line Name	**Laurel Corporation Statement of Cost of Goods Manufactured For Month Ended Aug. 31, 20--**	**Answers**
A. Cost of Goods Manufactured	$ 50,000.00	1. ______
B. Factory Overhead Applied	40,000.00	2. ______
C. Work in Process Inventory, Aug. 1, 20--	30,000.00	3. ______
D. Total Cost of Work in Process During August	$120,000.00	4. ______
E. Direct Labor	16,000.00	5. ______
F. Less Work in Process Inventory, Aug. 31, 20--	$136,000.00	6. ______
G. Total Cost of Work Placed in Process	12,000.00	7. ______
H. Direct Materials	$124,000.00	8. ______

© 2020 Cengage®. May not be scanned, copied or duplicated, or posted to a publicly accessible website, in whole or in part.

Part Four—Analyzing Transactions for a Manufacturing Business

Directions: For each entry below, print in the proper Answers column the letters identifying which accounts are to be debited and credited.

Account Titles	Transactions	Answers Debit	Answers Credit
A. Accounts Payable	**1.** Journalize entry for the month's indirect materials requisitions. (p. 503)	1. ______	______
B. Accumulated Depr.—Factory Equipment	**2.** Journalize entry for the month's direct materials requisitions. (p. 503)	2. ______	______
C. Cost of Goods Sold	**3.** Journalize entry for materials purchases. (p. 503)	3. ______	______
D. Depr. Expense—Factory Equipment	**4.** Journalize the end-of-period adjusting entry for factory equipment depreciation expense. (p. 509)	4. ______	______
E. Factory Equipment	**5.** Journalize entry for the month's applied factory overhead. (p. 510)	5. ______	______
F. Factory Overhead	**6.** Journalize entry to close the factory overhead account when there is overapplied overhead. (p. 510)	6. ______	______
G. Factory Payroll	**7.** Journalize entry to close the factory overhead account when there is underapplied overhead. (p. 510)	7. ______	______
H. Finished Goods	**8.** Journalize entry for the total of the finished goods manufactured during the month. (p. 513)	8. ______	______
I. Income Summary	**9.** Journalize entry for the month's cost of goods sold. (p. 513)	9. ______	______
J. Materials			
K. Work in Process			

© 2020 Cengage®. May not be scanned, copied or duplicated, or posted to a publicly accessible website, in whole or in part.

Name ______________________ Date ____________ Class ____________

17-1, 17-2, and 17-3 WORK TOGETHER, pp. 506, 511, and 518

17-1 Classifying manufacturing costs; recording and journalizing materials and labor costs (LO1, 2, 3, 4, 5, 6)
17-2 Completing a cost sheet and journalizing entries for overhead (LO7, 8)
17-3 Updating a finished goods ledger card; journalizing entries for finished goods and cost of goods sold (LO9, 10, 11)

17-1 (1.)

	Direct Materials	Direct Labor	Factory Overhead
a. Wood used to produce a desk			
b. Sandpaper used in production of a desk			
c. Cleaning solution for factory floors			
d. Wages earned by production employees			
e. Wages earned by factory maintenance worker			

2.

COST SHEET

Job. No. 218 Date April 15, 20--
Item G-78 Desk Date wanted May 15, 20--
No. of items 10 Date completed ____________
Ordered for Northland Furniture

DIRECT MATERIALS		DIRECT LABOR				SUMMARY	
REQ. NO.	AMOUNT	DATE	AMOUNT	DATE	AMOUNT	ITEM	AMOUNT
327	$ 95.00	Apr. 17	$120.00				
330	150.00	19	65.00				
332	300.00						

Extra space for calculations:

© 2020 Cengage®. May not be scanned, copied or duplicated, or posted to a publicly accessible website, in whole or in part.

3.

GENERAL JOURNAL PAGE 4

DATE		ACCOUNT TITLE	DOC. NO.	POST. REF.	DEBIT	CREDIT

© 2020 Cengage®. May not be scanned, copied or duplicated, or posted to a publicly accessible website, in whole or in part.

Name ______________________ Date ____________ Class ____________

17-1, 17-2, and 17-3 WORK TOGETHER (concluded)

CASH PAYMENTS JOURNAL

PAGE 8

	DATE		ACCOUNT TITLE	CK. NO.	POST. REF.	1 GENERAL DEBIT	2 GENERAL CREDIT	3 ACCOUNTS PAYABLE DEBIT	4 PURCHASES DISCOUNT CREDIT	5 CASH CREDIT	
1											1
2											2
3											3
4											4
5											5
6											6

FINISHED GOODS LEDGER CARD

Description Desk   Stock No. G-78

Minimum 5   Location Shelf 527B

MANUFACTURED/RECEIVED					SHIPPED/ISSUED					BALANCE			
DATE	JOB NO.	QUANTITY	UNIT COST	TOTAL COST	DATE	SALES INVOICE NO.	QUANTITY	UNIT COST	TOTAL COST	DATE	QUANTITY	UNIT COST	TOTAL COST
										20-- Apr. 1	25	170.00	4,250.00
					20-- Apr. 10	234	15	170.00					
							12	172.00	4,614.00	10	3	172.00	516.00

© 2020 Cengage®. May not be scanned, copied or duplicated, or posted to a publicly accessible website, in whole or in part.

17-1, 17-2, and 17-3 ON YOUR OWN, pp. 506, 511, 518

17-1 Classifying manufacturing costs; recording and journalizing materials and labor costs (LO1, 2, 3, 4, 5, 6)
17-2 Completing a cost sheet and journalizing entries for overhead (LO7, 8)
17-3 Updating a finished goods ledger card; journalizing entries for finished goods and cost of goods sold (LO9, 10, 11)

17-1 (1.)

	Direct Materials	Direct Labor	Factory Overhead
a. Fringe benefits of factory supervisor			
b. Factory property taxes			
c. Rivets used in production of grills			
d. Stainless steel for casing of grills			
e. Wages earned by production employees			

2.

COST SHEET

Job. No. 587 Date May 1, 20--
Item Model SS412 Date wanted June 3, 20--
No. of items 50 Date completed
Ordered for Stock

DIRECT MATERIALS		DIRECT LABOR				SUMMARY	
REQ. NO.	AMOUNT	DATE	AMOUNT	DATE	AMOUNT	ITEM	AMOUNT
410	$ 350.00	May 13	$ 650.00				
415	600.00	25	1,250.00				
418	548.00						

Extra space for calculations:

© 2020 Cengage®. May not be scanned, copied or duplicated, or posted to a publicly accessible website, in whole or in part.

Name ______________________ Date ____________ Class ____________

17-1, 17-2, and 17-3 ON YOUR OWN (continued)

GENERAL JOURNAL PAGE 5

DATE		ACCOUNT TITLE	DOC. NO.	POST. REF.	DEBIT	CREDIT

© 2020 Cengage®. May not be scanned, copied or duplicated, or posted to a publicly accessible website, in whole or in part.

3.

CASH PAYMENTS JOURNAL

PAGE 10

	DATE		ACCOUNT TITLE	CK. NO.	POST. REF.	GENERAL DEBIT (1)	GENERAL CREDIT (2)	ACCOUNTS PAYABLE DEBIT (3)	PURCHASES DISCOUNT CREDIT (4)	CASH CREDIT (5)	
1											1
2											2
3											3
4											4
5											5
6											6

FINISHED GOODS LEDGER CARD

Description Grill　　Stock No. SS412

Minimum 200　　Location Aisle 367; Shelf 2W

MANUFACTURED/RECEIVED					SHIPPED/ISSUED					BALANCE			
DATE	JOB NO.	QUANTITY	UNIT COST	TOTAL COST	DATE	SALES INVOICE NO.	QUANTITY	UNIT COST	TOTAL COST	DATE	QUANTITY	UNIT COST	TOTAL COST
										20-- May 1	450	125.50	56,475.00
					20-- May 5	575	115	130.25					
							10	134.00	16,318.75	5	175	134.00	23,450.00

© 2020 Cengage®. May not be scanned, copied or duplicated, or posted to a publicly accessible website, in whole or in part.

Name ______________________ Date ____________ Class ____________

17-4 WORK TOGETHER (LO14, 15, 16), p. 524

Calculating variances for materials and labor

1. Total Materials Variance =

Materials Price Variance =

Materials Quantity Variance =

© 2020 Cengage®. May not be scanned, copied or duplicated, or posted to a publicly accessible website, in whole or in part.

17-4 WORK TOGETHER (concluded)

2. Total Labor Variance =

Labor Price Variance =

Labor Quantity Variance =

© 2020 Cengage®. May not be scanned, copied or duplicated, or posted to a publicly accessible website, in whole or in part.

Name ______________________ Date ____________ Class ____________

17-4 ON YOUR OWN (LO14, 15, 16), p. 524

Calculating variances for materials and labor

1. Total Materials Variance =

Materials Price Variance =

Materials Quantity Variance =

© 2020 Cengage®. May not be scanned, copied or duplicated, or posted to a publicly accessible website, in whole or in part.

17-4 ON YOUR OWN (concluded)

2. Total Labor Variance =

Labor Price Variance =

Labor Quantity Variance =

© 2020 Cengage®. May not be scanned, copied or duplicated, or posted to a publicly accessible website, in whole or in part.

Name ______________________ Date ______________ Class ______________

17-1.1 APPLICATION PROBLEM (LO2, 3, 4), p. 526

Completing a materials ledger card and journalizing entries in a materials purchases journal

1.

MATERIALS LEDGER CARD

Article FL7500 Washer Tub Acct. No. 130

Reorder 200 Minimum 600 Location Bldg. 5; Aisle 58

ORDERED			RECEIVED					ISSUED					BALANCE			
DATE	PURCHASE ORDER NO.	QUANTITY	DATE	PURCHASE ORDER NO.	QUANTITY	UNIT PRICE	VALUE	DATE	REQUISITION NO.	QUANTITY	UNIT PRICE	VALUE	DATE	QUANTITY	UNIT PRICE	VALUE
													20-- Jan. 2	180	24.00	4,320.00

2.

MATERIALS PURCHASES JOURNAL PAGE 1

	DATE		ACCOUNT CREDITED	PURCH. NO.	POST. REF.	MATERIALS DR. ACCTS. PAY. CR.	
1							1
2							2
3							3
4							4
5							5
6							6

© 2020 Cengage®. May not be scanned, copied or duplicated, or posted to a publicly accessible website, in whole or in part.

17-1.2, 17-2, and 17-3.1 APPLICATION PROBLEM, pp. 526 and 527

17-1.2 Recording and journalizing materials and labor costs (LO2, 3, 4, 5, 6)
17-2 Completing a cost sheet and journalizing entries for overhead (LO7, 8)
17-3.1 Updating a finished goods ledger card; journalizing entries for finished goods and cost of goods sold (LO9, 10, 11)

COST SHEET

Job. No. 335 Date June 10, 20--
Item MEG3 Gear Date wanted June 30, 20--
No. of items 10,000 Date completed ______
Ordered for Stock

DIRECT MATERIALS		DIRECT LABOR				SUMMARY	
REQ. NO.	AMOUNT	DATE	AMOUNT	DATE	AMOUNT	ITEM	AMOUNT
212	$1,500.00	June 19	$2,950.00				
219	1,850.00	23	3,675.00				
224	1,250.00						

Extra space for calculations:

© 2020 Cengage®. May not be scanned, copied or duplicated, or posted to a publicly accessible website, in whole or in part.

Name ______________________ Date ______________ Class ______________

17-1.2, 17-2, and 17-3.1 APPLICATION PROBLEM (continued)

3.

GENERAL JOURNAL PAGE 4

DATE		ACCOUNT TITLE	DOC. NO.	POST. REF.	DEBIT	CREDIT

© 2020 Cengage®. May not be scanned, copied or duplicated, or posted to a publicly accessible website, in whole or in part.

CASH PAYMENTS JOURNAL

PAGE 8

					1	2	3	4	5	
	DATE	ACCOUNT TITLE	CK. NO.	POST. REF.	GENERAL DEBIT	GENERAL CREDIT	ACCOUNTS PAYABLE DEBIT	PURCHASES DISCOUNT CREDIT	CASH CREDIT	
1										1
2										2
3										3
4										4
5										5
6										6

FINISHED GOODS LEDGER CARD

Description Gear Stock No. MEG3

Minimum 50,000 Location Bin 1156

MANUFACTURED/RECEIVED					SHIPPED/ISSUED					BALANCE			
DATE	JOB NO.	QUANTITY	UNIT COST	TOTAL COST	DATE	SALES INVOICE NO.	QUANTITY	UNIT COST	TOTAL COST	DATE	QUANTITY	UNIT COST	TOTAL COST
										20-- June 1	60,000	1.95	117,000.00
					20-- June 10	366	16,000	1.98					
							11,000	1.99	53,570.00	10	45,000	1.99	89,550.00

© 2020 Cengage®. May not be scanned, copied or duplicated, or posted to a publicly accessible website, in whole or in part.

Name ______________________ Date ______________ Class ______________

17-3.2 APPLICATION PROBLEM (LO12, 13), p. 527

Preparing a statement of cost of goods manufactured and completing financial statements for a manufacturing business

1.

© 2020 Cengage®. May not be scanned, copied or duplicated, or posted to a publicly accessible website, in whole or in part.

2.

Medford Manufacturing

Partial Income Statement

For Month Ended April 30, 20--

			% OF NET SALES
Operating Revenue:			
Sales		712,458.00	100.0
Cost of Goods Sold:			
Finished Goods Inventory, April 1, 20--			
Cost of Goods Manufactured			
Total Cost of Finished Goods Available for Sale			
Less Finished Goods Inventory, April 30, 20--			
Cost of Goods Sold			
Overapplied Overhead			
Net Cost of Goods Sold			
Gross Profit on Operations			

© 2020 Cengage®. May not be scanned, copied or duplicated, or posted to a publicly accessible website, in whole or in part.

Name ______ Date ______ Class ______

17-3.2 APPLICATION PROBLEM (concluded)

3.

Medford Manufacturing

Partial Balance Sheet

April 30, 20--

ASSETS			
Current Assets:			
Cash		87,521.00	
Petty Cash		150.00	
Accounts Receivable	62,145.00		
Less Allowance for Uncollectible Accounts	3,100.00	59,045.00	
Materials			
Work in Process			
Finished Goods			
Supplies—Factory		4,521.00	
Supplies—Sales		3,368.00	
Supplies—Administrative		1,548.00	
Prepaid Insurance		1,800.00	
Total Current Assets			

© 2020 Cengage®. May not be scanned, copied or duplicated, or posted to a publicly accessible website, in whole or in part.

17-4 APPLICATION PROBLEM (LO15, 16), p. 528

Calculating variances for materials and labor

1. Total Materials Variance =

Materials Price Variance =

Materials Quantity Variance =

© 2020 Cengage®. May not be scanned, copied or duplicated, or posted to a publicly accessible website, in whole or in part.

Name ______________________ Date ____________ Class ____________

17-4 APPLICATION PROBLEM (concluded)

2. Total Labor Variance =

Labor Price Variance =

Labor Quantity Variance =

© 2020 Cengage®. May not be scanned, copied or duplicated, or posted to a publicly accessible website, in whole or in part.

17-M MASTERY PROBLEM (LO2, 3, 4, 5, 6, 7, 8, 9, 10, 11), p. 528

Preparing cost records and journalizing entries that summarize cost records at the end of a fiscal period

1.

2., 3.

COST SHEET

Job. No. ______ Date ______

Item ______ Date wanted ______

No. of items ______ Date completed ______

Ordered for ______

DIRECT MATERIALS		DIRECT LABOR				SUMMARY	
REQ. NO.	AMOUNT	DATE	AMOUNT	DATE	AMOUNT	ITEM	AMOUNT

© 2020 Cengage®. May not be scanned, copied or duplicated, or posted to a publicly accessible website, in whole or in part.

Name ____________ Date ________ Class ________

17-M MASTERY PROBLEM (continued)

4., 5., 6.

FINISHED GOODS LEDGER CARD

Description ____________ Stock No. ________

Minimum ____________ Location ________

MANUFACTURED/RECEIVED					SHIPPED/ISSUED					BALANCE			
DATE	JOB NO.	QUANTITY	UNIT COST	TOTAL COST	DATE	SALES INVOICE NO.	QUANTITY	UNIT COST	TOTAL COST	DATE	QUANTITY	UNIT COST	TOTAL COST

7.

CASH PAYMENTS JOURNAL PAGE 10

					1	2	3	4	5	
	DATE	ACCOUNT TITLE	CK. NO.	POST. REF.	GENERAL DEBIT	GENERAL CREDIT	ACCOUNTS PAYABLE DEBIT	PURCHASES DISCOUNT CREDIT	CASH CREDIT	
1										1
2										2
3										3
4										4
5										5
6										6

© 2020 Cengage®. May not be scanned, copied or duplicated, or posted to a publicly accessible website, in whole or in part.

17-M MASTERY PROBLEM (concluded)

8.–11.

GENERAL JOURNAL PAGE 5

	DATE		ACCOUNT TITLE	DOC. NO.	POST. REF.	DEBIT	CREDIT	
1								1
2								2
3								3
4								4
5								5
6								6
7								7
8								8
9								9
10								10
11								11
12								12
13								13
14								14
15								15
16								16
17								17
18								18
19								19
20								20
21								21
22								22
23								23
24								24
25								25
26								26
27								27
28								28
29								29
30								30
31								31

© 2020 Cengage®. May not be scanned, copied or duplicated, or posted to a publicly accessible website, in whole or in part.

Name ______________________ Date ______________ Class ______________

17-C CHALLENGE PROBLEM (LO7, 8), p. 530

Calculating overhead rate

1. (a)

1. (b)

1. (c)

2. (a)

2. (b)

2. (c)

© 2020 Cengage®. May not be scanned, copied or duplicated, or posted to a publicly accessible website, in whole or in part.

17-C CHALLENGE PROBLEM (concluded)

3.

4.

© 2020 Cengage®. May not be scanned, copied or duplicated, or posted to a publicly accessible website, in whole or in part.

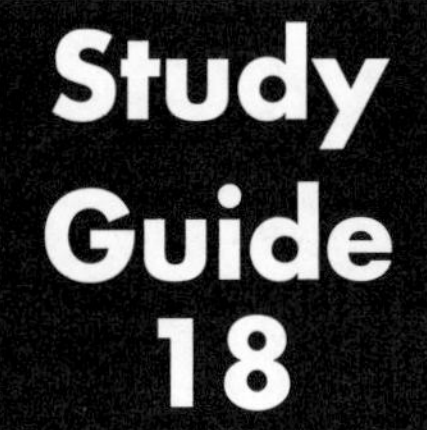

Name	Perfect Score	Your Score
Identifying Accounting Terms	17 Pts.	
Analyzing Business Decisions	15 Pts.	
Total	32 Pts.	

Part One—Identifying Accounting Terms

Directions: Select the one term in Column I that best fits each definition in Column II. Print the letter identifying your choice in the Answers column.

Column I	Column II	Answers
A. annuity	**1.** Analyzing only the differences between the revenues and expenses resulting from each of two options. (p. 534)	**1.** ______
B. compounding	**2.** Revenues that are different between two options. (p. 534)	**2.** ______
C. differential analysis	**3.** Costs that are different between two options. (p. 534)	**3.** ______
D. future value	**4.** A cost that occurred in the past and cannot be recovered by a future decision. (p. 534)	**4.** ______
E. future value of an annuity	**5.** Two or more products that are produced simultaneously with the same processes and costs and are inseparable up to a certain point. (p. 537)	**5.** ______
F. joint costs	**6.** The point where joint products are separable into identifiable products. (p. 537)	**6.** ______
G. joint products	**7.** The costs of processing joint products to their split-off point. (p. 537)	**7.** ______
H. net cash flows	**8.** The amount of time required to recover the cost of an investment. (p. 538)	**8.** ______
I. net present value	**9.** The expectation that invested money will increase over time. (p. 540)	**9** ______
J. payback period	**10.** The value of money invested today at some point in the future. (p. 541)	**10.** ______
K. present value	**11.** Earning interest on previously earned interest. (p. 541)	**11.** ______
L. present value of an annuity	**12.** The current value of a future cash payment or receipt. (p. 544)	**12.** ______
M. relevant costs	**13.** A series of equal cash flows. (p. 545)	**13.** ______
N. relevant revenues	**14.** The future value of an equal series of investments over equal time periods at a given interest rate. (p. 545)	**14.** ______
O. split-off point	**15.** An amount invested at a given interest rate that supports the payments of an annuity. (p. 546)	**15.** ______
P. sunk cost	**16.** The difference between the cash receipts and cash payments. (p. 548)	**16.** ______
Q. time value of money	**17.** The difference between the present value of the cash flows of the investment and the amount of the investment. (p. 548)	**17.** ______

© 2020 Cengage®. May not be scanned, copied or duplicated, or posted to a publicly accessible website, in whole or in part.

Part Two—Analyzing Business Decisions

Directions: Place a *T* for True or *F* for False in the Answers column to show whether each of the following statements is true or false.

	Answers
1. Depreciation incurred on an asset purchased several years ago is a sunk cost, which means it is also a relevant cost. (p. 534)	**1.** ______
2. Avoidable fixed overhead costs are relevant costs. (p. 535)	**2.** ______
3. In a special order decision, management can disregard the effect of the special order on normal sales. (p. 536)	**3.** ______
4. When deciding to discontinue a department, management must estimate the effect that discontinuing the department will have on sales for the remaining departments. (p. 537)	**4.** ______
5. Joint costs are sunk costs, which are always relevant. (p. 537)	**5.** ______
6. When using payback period to evaluate a decision, a shorter period is better than a longer period. (p. 538)	**6.** ______
7. The value of a dollar earned several years from now should be compared directly to the cost of the asset today. (p. 540)	**7.** ______
8. When calculating the future value of an investment, the interest earned each year is calculated by multiplying the investment value at the beginning of each year by the interest rate. (p. 541)	**8.** ______
9. The annual interest earned increases each year because of compounding interest. (p. 541)	**9.** ______
10. When making business decisions, all amounts must be precise, with no rounding allowed. (p. 544)	**10.** ______
11. While the time value of money is not critical for short-term decisions, it should be considered when making long-term decisions. (p. 548)	**11.** ______
12. When making decisions to purchase assets, managers expect to earn a specified percentage for the rate of return. (p. 548)	**12.** ______
13. If the desired rate of return is 5% and the net present value of an investment is negative, the investment is earning more than a 5% rate of return. (p. 548)	**13.** ______
14. Net present value can be calculated even if the investment has an unequal net cash flow. (p. 549)	**14.** ______
15. When considering a lease or buy decision, the additional net income and the additional repair and maintenance expenses are relevant. (p. 550)	**15.** ______

© 2020 Cengage®. May not be scanned, copied or duplicated, or posted to a publicly accessible website, in whole or in part.

Name ______________________ Date ____________ Class ____________

18-1 WORK TOGETHER (LO2, 4), p. 539

Determining relevant amounts

1.

Item	Relevant Amount	Irrelevant Amount
Direct materials		
Direct labor		
Variable overhead		
Fixed overhead		
Cost per unit to buy		

2.

Item	Relevant Amount	Irrelevant Amount
Sales		
Variable expenses		
Fixed costs		

© 2020 Cengage®. May not be scanned, copied or duplicated, or posted to a publicly accessible website, in whole or in part.

18-1 ON YOUR OWN (LO3, 5), p. 539

Determining relevant amounts

1.

Item	Relevant Amount	Irrelevant Amount
Sales revenue		
Direct materials		
Direct labor		
Variable overhead		
Fixed overhead		

2.

Item	Relevant Amount	Irrelevant Amount
Revenue		
Variable expenses		

© 2020 Cengage®. May not be scanned, copied or duplicated, or posted to a publicly accessible website, in whole or in part.

Name ______________________ Date ____________ Class ____________

18-2 WORK TOGETHER (LO8, 9, 10, 11), p. 547

Calculating future and present values

1.

Current value	
Future value factor (4 years, 6%)	
Future value	

2.

Future value	
Present value factor (5 years, 4%)	
Present value	

3.

Annuity amount	
Future value of an annuity factor (20 years, 8%)	
Future value	

____

____

4.

Annuity amount	
Present value of an annuity factor (4 years, 4%)	
Present value	

____

____

© 2020 Cengage®. May not be scanned, copied or duplicated, or posted to a publicly accessible website, in whole or in part.

18-2 ON YOUR OWN (LO8, 9, 10, 11), p. 547

Calculating future and present values

1.

Current value	
Future value factor (5 years, 10%)	
Future value	

2.

Future value	
Present value factor (6 years, 6%)	
Present value	

3.

Annuity amount	
Future value of an annuity factor (5 years, 8%)	
Future value	

____

____

4.

Annuity amount	
Present value of an annuity factor (20 years, 6%)	
Present value	

© 2020 Cengage®. May not be scanned, copied or duplicated, or posted to a publicly accessible website, in whole or in part.

Name ______________________ Date __________ Class __________

18-3 WORK TOGETHER (LO13, 14), p. 552

Using net present value to make business decisions

1.

Year	Net Cash Flows		Present Value Factor		Present Value of Net Cash Flows
1					
2					
3					
4					
5					
6					
Present value of net cash flows					
Investment					
Net present value					

____

____

____

2. Net cash flows, buying the machine:

	Now	Years 1–4	Year 4
Cost of machine			
Tax savings due to depreciation			
Sale of asset			
Net cash flows			

Present value of net cash flows, buying the machine:

Year	Net Cash Flows		Present Value of $1 Factor		Present Value of an Annuity Factor		Present Value of Net Cash Flows
0							
1–4							
4							
Present value of net cash flows							

© 2020 Cengage®. May not be scanned, copied or duplicated, or posted to a publicly accessible website, in whole or in part.

18-3 WORK TOGETHER (concluded)

Net cash flows, leasing the machine:

	Now	Years 1–4	Year 4
Lease payment, net of tax			
Net cash flows			

Present value of net cash flows, leasing the machine:

Year	Net Cash Flows		Present Value Factor		Present Value of an Annuity Factor		Present Value of Net Cash Flows
1–4							
Present value of net cash flows							

© 2020 Cengage®. May not be scanned, copied or duplicated, or posted to a publicly accessible website, in whole or in part.

Name ______________________ Date __________ Class __________

18-3 ON YOUR OWN (LO12, 14), p. 552

Using net present value to make business decisions

1.

Annual net cash flows	
Present value factor	
Present value of an annuity	
Investment	
Net present value	

____

____

____

____

2. Net cash flows, buying the machine:

	Now	Years 1–5	Year 5
Cost of machine			
Tax savings due to depreciation			
Sale of asset			
Net cash flows			

Present value of net cash flows, buying the machine:

Year	Net Cash Flows		Present Value of $1 Factor		Present Value of an Annuity Factor		Present Value of Net Cash Flows
0							
1–5							
5							
Present value of net cash flows							

© 2020 Cengage®. May not be scanned, copied or duplicated, or posted to a publicly accessible website, in whole or in part.

18-3 ON YOUR OWN (concluded)

Net cash flows, leasing the machine:

	Now	Years 1–5	Year 5
Lease payment, net of tax			
Net cash flows			

Present value of net cash flows, leasing the machine:

Year	Net Cash Flows		Present Value Factor		Present Value of an Annuity Factor		Present Value of Net Cash Flows
1–5							
Present value of net cash flows							

© 2020 Cengage®. May not be scanned, copied or duplicated, or posted to a publicly accessible website, in whole or in part.

Name ____________________ Date __________ Class __________

18-1.1 APPLICATION PROBLEM (LO2), p. 554

Calculations for a make or buy decision

	Make	Buy	Differential Analysis in Favor of Make
Direct materials			
Direct labor			
Variable overhead			
Fixed overhead			
Purchase price			

© 2020 Cengage®. May not be scanned, copied or duplicated, or posted to a publicly accessible website, in whole or in part.

18-1.2 APPLICATION PROBLEM (LO3), p. 554

Calculating relevant costs for a special order

	Accept Special Order	Reject Special Order	Differential Analysis in Favor of Acceptance
Sales revenue			
Direct materials			
Direct labor			
Variable overhead			
Special emblem			
Fixed costs			
Net increase			

© 2020 Cengage®. May not be scanned, copied or duplicated, or posted to a publicly accessible website, in whole or in part.

Name ______________________ Date ____________ Class ____________

18-1.3 APPLICATION PROBLEM (LO4), p. 554

Calculating relevant costs for a decision to discontinue a segment

	Keep Men's Clothing Department	Drop Men's Clothing Department	Differential Analysis in Favor of Keeping Men's Clothing Department
Sales			
Variable expenses			
Contribution margin			
Fixed costs			
Operating income			

© 2020 Cengage®. May not be scanned, copied or duplicated, or posted to a publicly accessible website, in whole or in part.

18-1.4 APPLICATION PROBLEM (LO5), p. 555

Calculating relevant costs for a sell or process further decision

	Process Further	Sell at Split-Off Point	Differential Analysis in Favor of Processing Further
Revenue			
Cost to process further			
Operating income			

© 2020 Cengage®. May not be scanned, copied or duplicated, or posted to a publicly accessible website, in whole or in part.

Name ______________________________ Date ____________ Class ____________

18-2 APPLICATION PROBLEM (LO8, 9, 10, 11), p. 555

Calculating future and present values

1.

Current value	
Future value factor	
Future value	

2. Present value of $65,000 today: ________

Present value of $100,000.00 five years from now:

Future value	
Present value factor	
Present value	

________ today has a higher present value.

3.

Annuity amount	
Future value of an annuity factor	
Future value	

The balance will be: ________

4.

Annuity amount	
Present value of an annuity factor	
Present value	

The present value of the offer: ________

© 2020 Cengage®. May not be scanned, copied or duplicated, or posted to a publicly accessible website, in whole or in part.

18-3 APPLICATION PROBLEM (LO12, 13, 14), p. 555

Using net present value to make business decisions

1.

Annual net cash flows	
Present value factor	
Present value of an annuity	
Investment	
Net present value	

2.

Year	Net Cash Flows		Present Value Factor		Present Value of Net Cash Flows
1					
2					
3					
4					
5					
Present value of net cash flows					
Investment					
Net present value					

3. Net cash flows, buying the machine:

	Now	Years 1–5	Year 5
Down payment			
Bond interest, net of tax savings			
Tax savings due to depreciation			
Retirement of bonds			
Sale of asset			
Net cash flows			

© 2020 Cengage®. May not be scanned, copied or duplicated, or posted to a publicly accessible website, in whole or in part.

18-3 APPLICATION PROBLEM (concluded)

Present value of net cash flows, buying the machine:

Year	Net Cash Flows		Present Value of $1 Factor		Present Value of an Annuity Factor		Present Value of Net Cash Flows
0							
1–5							
5							
Present value of net cash flows							

Net cash flows, leasing the machine:

	Now	Years 1–5	Year 5
Lease payment, net of tax			
New cash flows			

Present value of net cash flows, leasing the machine:

Year	Net Cash Flows		Present Value Factor		Present Value of an Annuity Factor		Present Value of Net Cash Flows

© 2020 Cengage®. May not be scanned, copied or duplicated, or posted to a publicly accessible website, in whole or in part.

18-M MASTERY PROBLEM (LO9, 13), p. 556

Calculating net present values

1. Abbott Industries

Year	Net Cash Flows		Present Value Factor		Present Value of Net Cash Flows
1					
2					
3					
4					
5					
6					
7					
Present value of net cash flows					
Investment					
Net present value					

Costello Manufacturing

Year	Net Cash Flows		Present Value Factor		Present Value of Net Cash Flows
1					
2					
3					
4					
5					
6					
7					
Present value of net cash flows					
Investment					
Net present value					

2. ____

© 2020 Cengage®. May not be scanned, copied or duplicated, or posted to a publicly accessible website, in whole or in part.

Name ______________________ Date ____________ Class ____________

18-C CHALLENGE PROBLEM (LO5), p. 556

Calculating relevant costs for a multiple product sell or process further decision

	Process into Extra-Lean Ground Beef	Process into Lean Ground Beef	Sell as Regular Ground Beef
Revenue			
Cost to process further			
Operating income			

____

____

____

____

____

© 2020 Cengage®. May not be scanned, copied or duplicated, or posted to a publicly accessible website, in whole or in part.

Name	Perfect Score	Your Score
Identifying Accounting Terms	14 Pts.	
Analyzing Process Costing, Activity-Based Costing, and Pricing Concepts	20 Pts.	
Analyzing Process Costing, Activity-Based Costing, and Pricing Practices	10 Pts.	
Total	44 Pts.	

Part One—Identifying Accounting Terms

Directions: Select the one term in Column I that best fits each definition in Column II. Print the letter identifying your choice in the Answers column.

Column I	*Column II*	*Answers*
A. activity rate	**1.** An estimate of the amount of direct materials, direct labor, and overhead that have already been incurred on partially finished units, stated in terms of fully completed units. (p. 561)	**1.** ______
B. activity-based costing (ABC)	**2.** The sum of the costs for direct labor and overhead. (p. 561)	**2.** ______
C. batch-level costs	**3.** A report that shows unit information and cost information for a department using a process costing system. (p. 564)	**3.** ______
D. conversion costs	**4.** Allocating factory overhead based on the level of major activities. (p. 567)	**4.** ______
E. cost driver	**5.** Resources used on activities connected with each individual unit produced. (p. 568)	**5.** ______
F. cost of production report	**6.** Resources used on activities connected with a group of products. (p. 568)	**6.** ______
G. cost pool	**7.** Resources used to support the entire product line. (p. 568)	**7.** ______
H. cost-based pricing	**8.** Resources used to support the entire company and production process. (p. 568)	**8.** ______
I. equivalent units of production (EUP)	**9.** A group of costs related to a specific activity. (p. 569)	**9.** ______
J. facility-sustaining level costs	**10.** The factor that affects the cost of an activity. (p. 569)	**10.** ______
K. product-level costs	**11.** A price for each unit of activity. (p. 569)	**11.** ______
L. target costing	**12.** A method of establishing a price for a product or service in which a fixed percentage or a fixed sum is added to the cost of the product or service. (p. 574)	**12.** ______
M. unit-level costs	**13.** A method of establishing a price for a product or service based on the value the product or service has to its customer. (p. 575)	**13.** ______
N. value-based pricing	**14.** A method of establishing a price for a product or service, based on the price the customer is willing to pay and controlling the cost of the product so that the company still makes a profit. (p. 575)	**14.** ______

© 2020 Cengage®. May not be scanned, copied or duplicated, or posted to a publicly accessible website, in whole or in part.

Part Two—Analyzing Process Costing, Activity-Based Costing, and Pricing Concepts

Directions: Place a *T* for True or *F* for False in the Answers column to show whether each of the following statements is true or false.

	Answers
1. Job order costing is used when a single process with a continuous flow of inputs produces the same product. (p. 560)	**1.** ______
2. When calculating equivalent units of production, total units processed must equal total units accounted for. (p. 561)	**2.** ______
3. In process costing, at the end of a period, the cost of finished goods is transferred from the final department to the Finished Goods account. (p. 563)	**3.** ______
4. A cost of production report is completed by each department. (p. 564)	**4.** ______
5. The bottom section of the cost of production report shows actual units and equivalent units of production. (p. 564)	**5.** ______
6. The cost of production report must be prepared using the first-in, first-out (FIFO) method. (p. 564)	**6.** ______
7. In process costing and job order costing, the predetermined overhead rate is commonly based on a cost element, such as direct labor hours, to which there is a direct connection. (p. 567)	**7.** ______
8. Inventory management is a unit-level cost. (p. 568)	**8.** ______
9. Machine setup is usually a batch-level cost. (p. 568)	**9.** ______
10. The number of machine setups each product requires is an example of a cost driver for the cost pool, machine setups. (p. 569)	**10.** ______
11. In an activity-based costing system, once activities are identified and a cost for each activity is determined, a company can use this information to identify inefficient activities. (p. 572)	**11.** ______
12. Activity-based costing is not recommended for use in service businesses. (p. 572)	**12.** ______
13. A disadvantage of activity-based costing is the initial cost and effort required to implement it. (p. 572)	**13.** ______
14. Activity-based costing conforms to generally accepted accounting principles (GAAP). (p. 572)	**14.** ______
15. The selling price of a product must be high enough to cover all of the costs of the product, the administrative expenses of the company, and an adequate profit. (p. 574)	**15.** ______
16. Cost-based product pricing is also known as *markup pricing*. (p. 574)	**16.** ______
17. Cost-based product pricing may lead to prices that are too high or too low. (p. 574)	**17.** ______
18. The percentage markup on a product is the same as the gross profit margin on that product. (p. 575)	**18.** ______
19. Target costing requires that management knows how much its customers are willing to pay for a product. (p. 575)	**19.** ______
20. Target costing is especially helpful when products are in the design stages. (p. 575)	**20.** ______

© 2020 Cengage®. May not be scanned, copied or duplicated, or posted to a publicly accessible website, in whole or in part.

Name ______________________ Date ____________ Class ____________

Part Three—Analyzing Process Costing, Activity-Based Costing, and Pricing Practices

Directions: For each of the following items, select the choice that best completes the statement. Print the letter identifying your choice in the Answers column.

Answers

1. If 10,000 units of a product are 40% complete as to conversion costs, the equivalent units of production (EUP) for conversion costs is (A) 10,000 units, (B) 6,000 units, (C) 4,000 units, (D) none of these. (p. 561) **1.** ______

2. If 10,000 units of a product are 100% complete as to direct materials, the EUP for direct materials is (A) 10,000 units, (B) 6,000 units, (C) 4,000 units, (D) none of these. (p. 561) **2.** ______

3. If units in the beginning work in process is 2,000, units started this period is 10,000, units completed this period is 9,000, and units in the ending work in process is 3,000, total units processed and units accounted for is (A) 24,000, (B) 15,000, (C) 12,000, (D) 8,000. (p. 562) **3.** ______

4. If the cost of goods transferred from the Processing Department to the Packaging Department is $150,000, the journal entry to record this transfer would include a (A) debit to Work in Process—Processing, (B) debit to Work in Process—Packaging, (C) a credit to Income Summary, (D) credit to Work in Process—Packaging. (p. 562) **4.** ______

5. On a cost of production report, if the current cost of direct materials is $50,000, the current cost of conversion is $20,000, the EUP as to direct materials is 10,000, and the EUP as to conversion is 5,000, the cost per unit for direct materials is (A) $7.00, (B) $5.00, (C) $4.67, (D) $4.00. (p. 564) **5.** ______

6. Assume that the activity cost for machine setups is $10,000.00 and the total activity usage for machine setups is 50. If product A requires 4 machine setups and product B requires 6 machine setups, the activity rate for machine setups is (A) $2,000.00, (B) $1,200.00, (C) $800.00, (D) $200.00. (p. 569) **6.** ______

7. Assume that the activity cost for machine setups is $10,000.00 and the total activity usage for machine setups is 50. If product A requires 4 machine setups and product B requires 6 machine setups, the machine setup cost allocated to product A is (A) $2,000.00, (B) $1,200.00, (C) $800.00, (D) $200.00. (p. 569) **7.** ______

8. If the total cost of a product is $150.00 and the company uses a 40% markup on its product, the selling price of the product is (A) $210.00, (B) $200.00, (C) $156.00, (D) $60.00. (p. 574) **8.** ______

9. If the total cost of a product is $150.00 and the company uses a 40% markup on its product, the gross profit margin of the product is (A) 40.00%, (B) 37.50%, (C) 28.57%, (D) none of these. (p. 574) **9.** ______

10. If customers are willing to pay $200.00 for a product and the company requires a 30% profit, the target cost of the product is (A) $320.00, (B) $260.00, (C) $170.00, (D) $140.00. (p. 575) **10.** ______

© 2020 Cengage®. May not be scanned, copied or duplicated, or posted to a publicly accessible website, in whole or in part.

Name ______________________ Date ____________ Class ____________

19-1 WORK TOGETHER (LO2, 3), p. 566

Calculating equivalent units of production and completing journal entries in process costing

1.

		Equivalent Units of Production	
	Actual Units	Direct Materials	Conversion Costs
Beginning WIP			
Units started			
Total units processed			
Beginning WIP (direct materials, 90% complete; conversion costs, 35% complete)			
Units started and completed			
Ending WIP (direct materials, 50% complete; conversion costs, 25% complete)			
Units accounted for			

2.

GENERAL JOURNAL PAGE 9

DATE		ACCOUNT TITLE	DOC. NO.	POST. REF.	DEBIT	CREDIT

© 2020 Cengage®. May not be scanned, copied or duplicated, or posted to a publicly accessible website, in whole or in part.

19-1 ON YOUR OWN (LO2, 3), p. 566

Calculating equivalent units of production and completing journal entries in process costing

1.

		Equivalent Units of Production	
	Actual Units	Direct Materials	Conversion Costs
Beginning WIP			
Units started			
Total units processed			
Beginning WIP (direct materials, 40% complete; conversion costs, 30% complete)			
Units started and completed			
Ending WIP (direct materials, 60% complete; conversion costs, 50% complete)			
Units accounted for			

2.

GENERAL JOURNAL PAGE 9

	DATE		ACCOUNT TITLE	DOC. NO.	POST. REF.	DEBIT	CREDIT	
22								22
23								23
24								24
25								25
26								26
27								27
28								28
29								29
30								30
31								31
32								32
33								33

© 2020 Cengage®. May not be scanned, copied or duplicated, or posted to a publicly accessible website, in whole or in part.

Name ______________________ Date ______________ Class ______________

19-2 WORK TOGETHER (LO6), p. 573

Calculating activity rates and allocating costs

1.

Activity Pool	Estimated Costs	Estimated Activity	Activity Rate
Preparing purchase orders	$ 50,000.00	25,000	
Receiving materials	100,000.00	100,000	
Storage of materials	10,000.00	50,000	
Issuing materials to production	200,000.00	20,000	

2.

Activity Pool	Activity Rate	Activity Amount	Allocated Costs
Preparing purchase orders			
Receiving materials			
Storage of materials			
Issuing materials to production			
Materials handling costs allocated			

© 2020 Cengage®. May not be scanned, copied or duplicated, or posted to a publicly accessible website, in whole or in part.

19-2 ON YOUR OWN (LO6), p. 573

Calculating activity rates and allocating costs

1.

Activity Pool	Estimated Costs	Estimated Activity	Activity Rate
Machine setups	$600,000.00	10,000	
Machine processing	200,000.00	50,000	
Shipping of product	75,000.00	25,000	

2.

Activity Pool	Activity Rate	Activity Amount	Allocated Costs
Machine setups			
Machine processing			
Shipping of product			
Allocated costs			

© 2020 Cengage®. May not be scanned, copied or duplicated, or posted to a publicly accessible website, in whole or in part.

Name ______________________________ Date ______________ Class ______________

19-3 WORK TOGETHER (LO8, 9), p. 576

Calculating cost-based pricing and target costs

1.

Item	Cost	Percentage Markup	Dollar Markup	Selling Price	Profit Margin
Dining table	$750.00	125%			
Recliner	425.00	75%			
Side table	60.00	50%			

2. Target Cost =

© 2020 Cengage®. May not be scanned, copied or duplicated, or posted to a publicly accessible website, in whole or in part.

19-3 ON YOUR OWN (LO8, 9), p. 576

Calculating cost-based pricing and target costs

1.

Item	Cost	Percentage Markup	Dollar Markup	Selling Price	Profit Margin
Men's watch	$ 50.00	40%			
Women's watch	45.00	40%			
Necklace	125.00	80%			
Bracelet	75.00	80%			

2. Target Cost =

© 2020 Cengage®. May not be scanned, copied or duplicated, or posted to a publicly accessible website, in whole or in part.

Name ______________________ Date ____________ Class ____________

19-1 APPLICATION PROBLEM (LO2, 3), p. 578

Calculating equivalent units of production and completing journal entries in process costing

1.

		Equivalent Units of Production	
	Actual Units	Direct Materials	Conversion Costs
Beginning WIP			
Units started			
Total units processed			
Beginning WIP (direct materials, 80% complete; conversion costs, 40% complete)			
Units started and completed			
Ending WIP (direct materials, 70% complete; conversion costs, 30% complete)			
Units accounted for			

2.

GENERAL JOURNAL PAGE 9

	DATE		ACCOUNT TITLE	DOC. NO.	POST. REF.	DEBIT	CREDIT	
25								25
26								26
27								27
28								28
29								29
30								30
31								31
32								32
33								33
34								34
35								35
36								36

© 2020 Cengage®. May not be scanned, copied or duplicated, or posted to a publicly accessible website, in whole or in part.

19-2 APPLICATION PROBLEM (LO6), p. 578

Calculating activity rates and allocating costs

1.

Activity Pool	Estimated Costs	Estimated Activity	Activity Rate
Cutting machine setups	$400,000.00	10,000	
Cutting machine usage	500,000.00	125,000	
Moving	200,000.00	400,000	
Storage	440,000.00	2,200,000	
Assembly	400,000.00	40,000	

2.

Activity Pool	Activity Rate	Activity Amount	Allocated Costs

© 2020 Cengage®. May not be scanned, copied or duplicated, or posted to a publicly accessible website, in whole or in part.

Name ______________________________ Date ______________ Class ______________

19-3 APPLICATION PROBLEM (LO8, 9), p. 579

Calculating cost-based pricing and target costs

1.

Item	Cost	Percentage Markup	Dollar Markup	Selling Price	Profit Margin
Carry-on	$22.00	75%			
26-inch	44.00	70%			
32-inch	65.00	80%			

2. Target Cost =

© 2020 Cengage®. May not be scanned, copied or duplicated, or posted to a publicly accessible website, in whole or in part.

19-M MASTERY PROBLEM (LO2, 3, 8, 9), p. 579

Calculating equivalent units of production and completing journal entries in process costing

1.

		Equivalent Units of Production	
	Actual Units	Direct Materials	Conversion Costs
Beginning WIP			
Units started			
Total units processed			
Beginning WIP (direct materials, 100% complete; conversion costs, 30% complete)			
Units started and completed			
Ending WIP (direct materials, 100% complete; conversion costs, 60% complete)			
Units accounted for			

2.

GENERAL JOURNAL PAGE 9

	DATE	ACCOUNT TITLE	DOC. NO.	POST. REF.	DEBIT	CREDIT	
22							22
23							23
24							24
25							25
26							26
27							27
28							28
29							29
30							30
31							31
32							32
33							33

© 2020 Cengage®. May not be scanned, copied or duplicated, or posted to a publicly accessible website, in whole or in part.

19-M MASTERY PROBLEM (concluded)

3.

Item	Cost	Percentage Markup	Dollar Markup	Selling Price	Profit Margin
Ketchup		20%			

4. Target Cost =

© 2020 Cengage®. May not be scanned, copied or duplicated, or posted to a publicly accessible website, in whole or in part.

19-C CHALLENGE PROBLEM (LO6), p. 580

Activity-based costing in a service business

1.

Activity Pool	Estimated Costs	Estimated Activity	Activity Rate
Patient intake processing			
X-rays			
CT scan—scans			
CT scan—minutes			
MRI—images			
MRI—minutes			

2a. Patient No. 03016598

Activity Pool	Activity Rate	Activity Amount	Allocated Costs

2b. Patient No. 10415423

Activity Pool	Activity Rate	Activity Amount	Allocated Costs

© 2020 Cengage®. May not be scanned, copied or duplicated, or posted to a publicly accessible website, in whole or in part.

Name ____________________ Date ____________ Class ____________

REINFORCEMENT ACTIVITY 4, p. 582

Processing and Analyzing Cost Accounting Data for a Manufacturing Business

1.

2., 4.

MATERIALS PURCHASES JOURNAL PAGE

	DATE		ACCOUNT CREDITED	PURCH. NO.	POST. REF.	MATERIALS DR. ACCTS. PAY. CR.	
1							1
2							2
3							3
4							4
5							5
6							6
7							7
8							8
9							9
10							10
11							11
12							12
13							13
14							14
15							15
16							16
17							17
18							18
19							19
20							20
21							21
22							22
23							23
24							24
25							25
26							26

© 2020 Cengage®. May not be scanned, copied or duplicated, or posted to a publicly accessible website, in whole or in part.

REINFORCEMENT ACTIVITY 4 (continued)

2., 5.

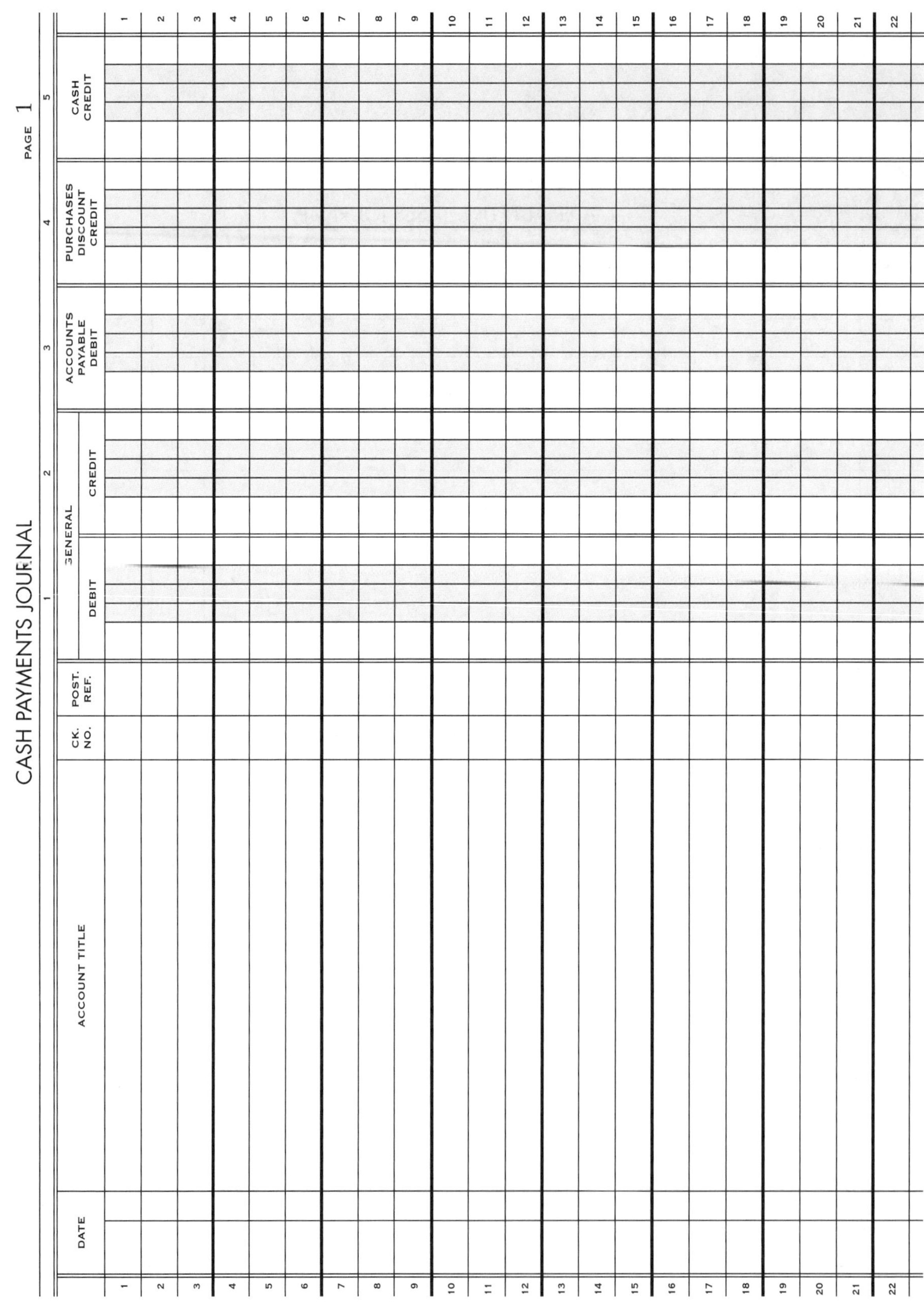

© 2020 Cengage®. May not be scanned, copied or duplicated, or posted to a publicly accessible website, in whole or in part.

Name ______________________ Date ____________ Class ____________

REINFORCEMENT ACTIVITY 4 (continued)

GENERAL JOURNAL

PAGE 1

DATE		ACCOUNT TITLE	DOC. NO.	POST. REF.	DEBIT	CREDIT

© 2020 Cengage®. May not be scanned, copied or duplicated, or posted to a publicly accessible website, in whole or in part.

REINFORCEMENT ACTIVITY 4 (continued)

4., 6., 7., 8.

GENERAL LEDGER

ACCOUNT Materials ACCOUNT NO. 1125

DATE		ITEM	POST. REF.	DEBIT	CREDIT	BALANCE DEBIT	BALANCE CREDIT
20-- Jan.	1	Balance	✔			40 0 9 6 00	

ACCOUNT Work in Process ACCOUNT NO. 1130

DATE		ITEM	POST. REF.	DEBIT	CREDIT	BALANCE DEBIT	BALANCE CREDIT

ACCOUNT Finished Goods ACCOUNT NO. 1135

DATE		ITEM	POST. REF.	DEBIT	CREDIT	BALANCE DEBIT	BALANCE CREDIT
20-- Jan.	1	Balance	✔			86 3 8 0 00	

ACCOUNT Accounts Payable ACCOUNT NO. 2105

DATE		ITEM	POST. REF.	DEBIT	CREDIT	BALANCE DEBIT	BALANCE CREDIT
20-- Jan.	31	Balance	✔			23 5 4 4 80	

© 2020 Cengage®. May not be scanned, copied or duplicated, or posted to a publicly accessible website, in whole or in part.

Name ______________________ Date __________ Class __________

REINFORCEMENT ACTIVITY 4 (continued)

ACCOUNT Employee Income Tax Payable ACCOUNT NO. 2110

DATE		ITEM	POST. REF.	DEBIT	CREDIT	BALANCE DEBIT	BALANCE CREDIT
20-- Jan.	31	Balance	✔				3 248 20

ACCOUNT Social Security Tax Payable ACCOUNT NO. 2120

DATE		ITEM	POST. REF.	DEBIT	CREDIT	BALANCE DEBIT	BALANCE CREDIT
20-- Jan.	31	Balance	✔				3 708 42

ACCOUNT Medicare Tax Payable ACCOUNT NO. 2125

DATE		ITEM	POST. REF.	DEBIT	CREDIT	BALANCE DEBIT	BALANCE CREDIT
20-- Jan.	31	Balance	✔				855 78

ACCOUNT Unemployment Tax Payable—Federal ACCOUNT NO. 2130

DATE		ITEM	POST. REF.	DEBIT	CREDIT	BALANCE DEBIT	BALANCE CREDIT
20-- Jan.	31	Balance	✔				228 10

© 2020 Cengage®. May not be scanned, copied or duplicated, or posted to a publicly accessible website, in whole or in part.

REINFORCEMENT ACTIVITY 4 (continued)

ACCOUNT Unemployment Tax Payable—State ACCOUNT NO. 2135

DATE		ITEM	POST. REF.	DEBIT	CREDIT	BALANCE DEBIT	BALANCE CREDIT
20-- Jan.	31	Balance	✔				1 540 42

ACCOUNT Income Summary ACCOUNT NO. 3120

DATE		ITEM	POST. REF.	DEBIT	CREDIT	BALANCE DEBIT	BALANCE CREDIT

ACCOUNT Cost of Goods Sold ACCOUNT NO. 5105

DATE		ITEM	POST. REF.	DEBIT	CREDIT	BALANCE DEBIT	BALANCE CREDIT

ACCOUNT Factory Overhead ACCOUNT NO. 5505

DATE		ITEM	POST. REF.	DEBIT	CREDIT	BALANCE DEBIT	BALANCE CREDIT

© 2020 Cengage®. May not be scanned, copied or duplicated, or posted to a publicly accessible website, in whole or in part.

Name ______ Date ______ Class ______

REINFORCEMENT ACTIVITY 4 (continued)

ACCOUNT Depreciation Expense—Factory Equipment ACCOUNT NO. 5510

DATE		ITEM	POST. REF.	DEBIT	CREDIT	BALANCE DEBIT	BALANCE CREDIT
20-- Jan.	31	Balance	✔			4 392 00	

ACCOUNT Depreciation Expense—Building ACCOUNT NO. 5515

DATE		ITEM	POST. REF.	DEBIT	CREDIT	BALANCE DEBIT	BALANCE CREDIT
20-- Jan.	31	Balance	✔			2 306 00	

ACCOUNT Heat, Light, and Power Expense ACCOUNT NO. 5520

DATE		ITEM	POST. REF.	DEBIT	CREDIT	BALANCE DEBIT	BALANCE CREDIT
20-- Jan.	31	Balance	✔			10 488 40	

ACCOUNT Insurance Expense—Factory ACCOUNT NO. 5525

DATE		ITEM	POST. REF.	DEBIT	CREDIT	BALANCE DEBIT	BALANCE CREDIT
20-- Jan.	31	Balance	✔			384 00	

ACCOUNT Miscellaneous Expense—Factory ACCOUNT NO. 5530

DATE		ITEM	POST. REF.	DEBIT	CREDIT	BALANCE DEBIT	BALANCE CREDIT
20-- Jan.	31	Balance	✔			940 94	

© 2020 Cengage®. May not be scanned, copied or duplicated, or posted to a publicly accessible website, in whole or in part.

REINFORCEMENT ACTIVITY 4 (continued)

ACCOUNT Payroll Taxes Expense—Factory ACCOUNT NO. 5535

DATE		ITEM	POST. REF.	DEBIT	CREDIT	BALANCE DEBIT	BALANCE CREDIT

ACCOUNT Property Tax Expense—Factory ACCOUNT NO. 5540

DATE		ITEM	POST. REF.	DEBIT	CREDIT	BALANCE DEBIT	BALANCE CREDIT
20-- Jan.	31	Balance	✔			1 319 60	

ACCOUNT Supplies Expense—Factory ACCOUNT NO. 5545

DATE		ITEM	POST. REF.	DEBIT	CREDIT	BALANCE DEBIT	BALANCE CREDIT
20-- Jan.	31	Balance	✔			2 970 50	

© 2020 Cengage®. May not be scanned, copied or duplicated, or posted to a publicly accessible website, in whole or in part.

Name ____________________ Date ____________ Class ____________

REINFORCEMENT ACTIVITY 4 (continued)

MATERIALS LEDGER CARD

Article Resin Acct. No. 110

Reorder 30,000 Minimum 10,000 Location B10

ORDERED			RECEIVED					ISSUED					BALANCE			
DATE	PURCHASE ORDER NO.	QUANTITY	DATE	PURCHASE ORDER NO.	QUANTITY	UNIT PRICE	VALUE	DATE	REQUISITION NO.	QUANTITY	UNIT PRICE	VALUE	DATE	QUANTITY	UNIT PRICE	VALUE
													20-- Jan. 1	18,000	0.40	7,200.00

© 2020 Cengage®. May not be scanned, copied or duplicated, or posted to a publicly accessible website, in whole or in part.

REINFORCEMENT ACTIVITY 4 (continued)

MATERIALS LEDGER CARD

Article Polymer Acct. No. 120

Reorder 20,000 Minimum 10,000 Location B20

ORDERED			RECEIVED						ISSUED					BALANCE			
DATE	PURCHASE ORDER NO.	QUANTITY	DATE	PURCHASE ORDER NO.	QUANTITY	UNIT PRICE	VALUE	DATE	REQUISITION NO.	QUANTITY	UNIT PRICE	VALUE	DATE	QUANTITY	UNIT PRICE	VALUE
													20-- Jan. 1	17,000	1.20	20,400.00

© 2020 Cengage®. May not be scanned, copied or duplicated, or posted to a publicly accessible website, in whole or in part.

Name ______________________ Date ______________ Class ______________

REINFORCEMENT ACTIVITY 4 (continued)

MATERIALS LEDGER CARD

Article Dye Acct. No. 210

Reorder 1,000 Minimum 520 Location C10

ORDERED			RECEIVED					ISSUED					BALANCE			
DATE	PURCHASE ORDER NO.	QUANTITY	DATE	PURCHASE ORDER NO.	QUANTITY	UNIT PRICE	VALUE	DATE	REQUISITION NO.	QUANTITY	UNIT PRICE	VALUE	DATE	QUANTITY	UNIT PRICE	VALUE
													20-- Jan. 1	830.0	3.20	2,656.00

© 2020 Cengage®. May not be scanned, copied or duplicated, or posted to a publicly accessible website, in whole or in part.

MATERIALS LEDGER CARD

Article Connectors　　　Acct. No. 310

Reorder 1,600　　　Minimum 800　　　Location D10

ORDERED			RECEIVED					ISSUED					BALANCE			
DATE	PURCHASE ORDER NO.	QUANTITY	DATE	PURCHASE ORDER NO.	QUANTITY	UNIT PRICE	VALUE	DATE	REQUI-SITION NO.	QUANTITY	UNIT PRICE	VALUE	DATE	QUANTITY	UNIT PRICE	VALUE
													20-- Jan. 1	1,800	2.50	4,500.00

© 2020 Cengage®. May not be scanned, copied or duplicated, or posted to a publicly accessible website, in whole or in part.

Name ______________________ Date ____________ Class ____________

REINFORCEMENT ACTIVITY 4 (continued)

MATERIALS LEDGER CARD

Article Metal Glides (set of 2) Acct. No. 320

Reorder 300 Minimum 100 Location D20

ORDERED			RECEIVED					ISSUED					BALANCE			
DATE	PURCHASE ORDER NO.	QUANTITY	DATE	PURCHASE ORDER NO.	QUANTITY	UNIT PRICE	VALUE	DATE	REQUISITION NO.	QUANTITY	UNIT PRICE	VALUE	DATE	QUANTITY	UNIT PRICE	VALUE
													20-- Jan. 1	300	2.00	600.00

© 2020 Cengage®. May not be scanned, copied or duplicated, or posted to a publicly accessible website, in whole or in part.

MATERIALS LEDGER CARD

Article Hinges (set of 2) Acct. No. 330

Reorder 1,000 Minimum 300 Location D30

ORDERED			RECEIVED					ISSUED					BALANCE			
DATE	PURCHASE ORDER NO.	QUANTITY	DATE	PURCHASE ORDER NO.	QUANTITY	UNIT PRICE	VALUE	DATE	REQUISITION NO.	QUANTITY	UNIT PRICE	VALUE	DATE	QUANTITY	UNIT PRICE	VALUE
													20-- Jan. 1	600	2.00	1,200.00

© 2020 Cengage®. May not be scanned, copied or duplicated, or posted to a publicly accessible website, in whole or in part.

Name ______ Date ______ Class ______

REINFORCEMENT ACTIVITY 4 (continued)

MATERIALS LEDGER CARD

Article Fasteners — Acct. No. 340

Reorder 1,000 — Minimum 600 — Location D40

ORDERED			RECEIVED					ISSUED					BALANCE			
DATE	PURCHASE ORDER NO.	QUANTITY	DATE	PURCHASE ORDER NO.	QUANTITY	UNIT PRICE	VALUE	DATE	REQUISITION NO.	QUANTITY	UNIT PRICE	VALUE	DATE	QUANTITY	UNIT PRICE	VALUE
													20-- Jan. 1	560	1.50	840.00

© 2020 Cengage®. May not be scanned, copied or duplicated, or posted to a publicly accessible website, in whole or in part.

2., 3., 10.

COST SHEET

Job. No. ____________ Date ____________

Item ____________ Date wanted ____________

No. of items ____________ Date completed ____________

Ordered for ____________

DIRECT MATERIALS		DIRECT LABOR				SUMMARY	
REQ. NO.	AMOUNT	DATE	AMOUNT	DATE	AMOUNT	ITEM	AMOUNT

COST SHEET

Job. No. ____________ Date ____________

Item ____________ Date wanted ____________

No. of items ____________ Date completed ____________

Ordered for ____________

DIRECT MATERIALS		DIRECT LABOR				SUMMARY	
REQ. NO.	AMOUNT	DATE	AMOUNT	DATE	AMOUNT	ITEM	AMOUNT

© 2020 Cengage®. May not be scanned, copied or duplicated, or posted to a publicly accessible website, in whole or in part.

REINFORCEMENT ACTIVITY 4 (continued)

COST SHEET

Job. No. ______________________ Date ______________________

Item ______________________ Date wanted ______________________

No. of items ______________________ Date completed ______________________

Ordered for ______________________

DIRECT MATERIALS		DIRECT LABOR				SUMMARY	
REQ. NO.	AMOUNT	DATE	AMOUNT	DATE	AMOUNT	ITEM	AMOUNT

COST SHEET

Job. No. ______________________ Date ______________________

Item ______________________ Date wanted ______________________

No. of items ______________________ Date completed ______________________

Ordered for ______________________

DIRECT MATERIALS		DIRECT LABOR				SUMMARY	
REQ. NO.	AMOUNT	DATE	AMOUNT	DATE	AMOUNT	ITEM	AMOUNT

© 2020 Cengage®. May not be scanned, copied or duplicated, or posted to a publicly accessible website, in whole or in part.

REINFORCEMENT ACTIVITY 4 (continued)

COST SHEET

Job. No. ______________ Date ______________

Item ______________ Date wanted ______________

No. of items ______________ Date completed ______________

Ordered for ______________

DIRECT MATERIALS		DIRECT LABOR				SUMMARY	
REQ. NO.	AMOUNT	DATE	AMOUNT	DATE	AMOUNT	ITEM	AMOUNT

COST SHEET

Job. No. ______________ Date ______________

Item ______________ Date wanted ______________

No. of items ______________ Date completed ______________

Ordered for ______________

DIRECT MATERIALS		DIRECT LABOR				SUMMARY	
REQ. NO.	AMOUNT	DATE	AMOUNT	DATE	AMOUNT	ITEM	AMOUNT

© 2020 Cengage®. May not be scanned, copied or duplicated, or posted to a publicly accessible website, in whole or in part.

REINFORCEMENT ACTIVITY 4 (continued)

COST SHEET

Job. No. ____________ Date ____________

Item ____________ Date wanted ____________

No. of items ____________ Date completed ____________

Ordered for ____________

DIRECT MATERIALS		DIRECT LABOR				SUMMARY	
REQ. NO.	AMOUNT	DATE	AMOUNT	DATE	AMOUNT	ITEM	AMOUNT

© 2020 Cengage®. May not be scanned, copied or duplicated, or posted to a publicly accessible website, in whole or in part.

2., 10.

FINISHED GOODS LEDGER CARD

Description Book Rack   Stock No. C200

Minimum 100   Location J10

MANUFACTURED/RECEIVED					SHIPPED/ISSJED					BALANCE			
DATE	JOB NO.	QUANTITY	UNIT COST	TOTAL COST	DATE	SALES INVOICE NO.	QUANTITY	UNIT COST	TOTAL COST	DATE	QUANTITY	UNIT COST	TOTAL COST
										20-- Jan. 1	150	130.00	19,500.00

© 2020 Cengage®. May not be scanned, copied or duplicated, or posted to a publicly accessible website, in whole or in part.

Name ______________________ Date ____________ Class ____________

REINFORCEMENT ACTIVITY 4 (continued)

FINISHED GOODS LEDGER CARD

Description Shelving Unit Stock No. P150

Minimum 50 Location J20

MANUFACTURED/RECEIVED					SHIPPED/ISSUED					BALANCE			
DATE	JOB NO.	QUANTITY	UNIT COST	TOTAL COST	DATE	SALES INVOICE NO.	QUANTITY	UNIT COST	TOTAL COST	DATE	QUANTITY	UNIT COST	TOTAL COST
										20-- Jan. 1	50	110.00	5,500.00

© 2020 Cengage®. May not be scanned, copied or duplicated, or posted to a publicly accessible website, in whole or in part.

FINISHED GOODS LEDGER CARD

Description Inline Skate Boot　　Stock No. E400

Minimum 50　　Location K10

MANUFACTURED/RECEIVED					SHIPPED/ISSUED					BALANCE			
DATE	JOB NO.	QUANTITY	UNIT COST	TOTAL COST	DATE	SALES INVOICE NO.	QUANTITY	UNIT COST	TOTAL COST	DATE	QUANTITY	UNIT COST	TOTAL COST
										20-- Jan. 1	40	220.00	8,800.00

© 2020 Cengage®. May not be scanned, copied or duplicated, or posted to a publicly accessible website, in whole or in part.

Name ______________________ Date ____________ Class ____________

REINFORCEMENT ACTIVITY 4 (continued)

FINISHED GOODS LEDGER CARD

Description Bench Stock No. V110

Minimum 200 Location K20

MANUFACTURED/RECEIVED					SHIPPED/ISSUED					BALANCE			
DATE	JOB NO.	QUANTITY	UNIT COST	TOTAL COST	DATE	SALES INVOICE NO.	QUANTITY	UNIT COST	TOTAL COST	DATE	QUANTITY	UNIT COST	TOTAL COST
										20-- Jan. 1	350	102.00	35,700.00

© 2020 Cengage®. May not be scanned, copied or duplicated, or posted to a publicly accessible website, in whole or in part.

FINISHED GOODS LEDGER CARD

Description Vertical Bookcase — Stock No. B160

Minimum 50 — Location L10

MANUFACTURED/RECEIVED					SHIPPED/ISSUED					BALANCE			
DATE	JOB NO.	QUANTITY	UNIT COST	TOTAL COST	DATE	SALES INVOICE NO.	QUANTITY	UNIT COST	TOTAL COST	DATE	QUANTITY	UNIT COST	TOTAL COST
										20-- Jan. 1	60	172.00	10,320.00

© 2020 Cengage®. May not be scanned, copied or duplicated, or posted to a publicly accessible website, in whole or in part.

Name ____________ Date ____________ Class ____________

REINFORCEMENT ACTIVITY 4 (continued)

FINISHED GOODS LEDGER CARD

Description Serving Cart Stock No. T120

Minimum 25 Location L20

MANUFACTURED/RECEIVED					SHIPPED/ISSUED					BALANCE			
DATE	JOB NO.	QUANTITY	UNIT COST	TOTAL COST	DATE	SALES INVOICE NO.	QUANTITY	UNIT COST	TOTAL COST	DATE	QUANTITY	UNIT COST	TOTAL COST
										20-- Jan. 1	80	82.00	6,560.00

© 2020 Cengage®. May not be scanned, copied or duplicated, or posted to a publicly accessible website, in whole or in part.

REINFORCEMENT ACTIVITY 4 (continued)

10.

Direct and Indirect Materials Ledger Proof	Cost Ledger Proof	Finished Goods Ledger Proof

11.

Alexandria Corporation

Statement of Cost of Goods Manufactured

For Month Ended January 31, 20--

Direct Materials		
Direct Labor		
Factory Overhead Applied		
Total Cost of Work Placed in Process		
Work in Process Inventory, January 1, 20--		
Total Cost of Work in Process During January		
Less Work in Process Inventory, January 31, 20--		
Cost of Good Manufactured		

© 2020 Cengage®. May not be scanned, copied or duplicated, or posted to a publicly accessible website, in whole or in part.

REINFORCEMENT ACTIVITY 4 (continued)

12.

a. Total Labor Variance =

b. Labor Price Variance =

c. Labor Quantity Variance =

© 2020 Cengage®. May not be scanned, copied or duplicated, or posted to a publicly accessible website, in whole or in part.

REINFORCEMENT ACTIVITY 4 (continued)

13.

	Make	Buy	Differential Analysis in Favor of Make
Direct materials			
Direct labor			
Variable overhead			
Fixed overhead			
Purchase price			

14.

Annual net cash flows	
Present value factor	
Present value of an annuity	
Investment	
Net present value	

15.

Item	Cost	Percentage Markup	Dollar Markup	Selling Price	Profit Margin
P150 Shelving unit		30%			
E400 Inline skate boot		40%			
V110 Bench		30%			
T120 Serving cart		50%			

© 2020 Cengage®. May not be scanned, copied or duplicated, or posted to a publicly accessible website, in whole or in part.

Name ______________________ Date ______________ Class ______________

REINFORCEMENT ACTIVITY 4 (concluded)

16.

Target Cost =

17.

© 2020 Cengage®. May not be scanned, copied or duplicated, or posted to a publicly accessible website, in whole or in part.

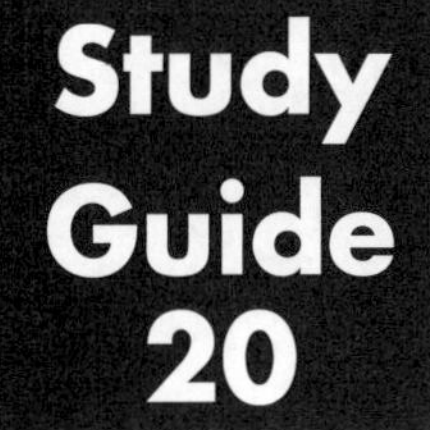

Name	Perfect Score	Your Score
Analyzing Concepts of Internal Control	17 Pts.	
Analyzing Voucher Transactions	15 Pts.	
Identifying Accounting Terms	26 Pts.	
Total	58 Pts.	

Part One—Analyzing Concepts of Internal Control

Directions: Place a *T* for True or an *F* for False in the Answers column to show whether each of the following statements is true or false.

		Answers
1.	Properly designed internal controls provide absolute assurance that a transaction is recorded accurately. (p. 592)	**1.** ______
2.	Cash and inventory are common targets of occupational fraud. (p. 593)	**2.** ______
3.	Overstating expenses is the most common form of financial statement misstatement. (p. 593)	**3.** ______
4.	A corporation should have a code of conduct and regularly train its employees on how to make ethical decisions. (p. 593)	**4.** ______
5.	Having internal auditors observe procedures and collect information to ensure that policies are being followed is a part of the control environment. (p. 593)	**5.** ______
6.	The Sarbanes-Oxley Act requires management to assess the quality of its internal controls. (p. 594)	**6.** ______
7.	Segregation of duties requires that two or more employees be involved in every transaction. (p. 594)	**7.** ______
8.	Bold lines on a flowchart segregate the tasks of each primary employee, department, or external party. (p. 597)	**8.** ______
9.	A business should flowchart the process of a system on a single page. (p. 597)	**9.** ______
10.	A flowchart should include the identification of key controls and risks. (pp. 597–599)	**10.** ______
11.	To reduce the chance of errors, the same employee should prepare the requisition and purchase order. (p. 602)	**11.** ______
12.	The voucher consists of a requisition, purchase order, receiving report, and invoice of the transaction. (p. 602)	**12.** ______
13.	Similar to a purchases journal, a voucher register has special columns that are used to record certain transactions. (p. 603)	**13.** ______
14.	For proper control of cash expenditures, the check signer should return the signed check to the Accounts Payable Department. (p. 605)	**14.** ______
15.	A check register does not have a General Debit or General Credit column. (p. 606)	**15.** ______
16.	A voucher system should not be modified to meet the needs of the business. (p. 608)	**16.** ______
17.	Documentation is critical in helping accountants understand and evaluate accounting systems. (p. 608)	**17.** ______

© 2020 Cengage®. May not be scanned, copied or duplicated, or posted to a publicly accessible website, in whole or in part.

Part Two—Analyzing Voucher Transactions

Directions: Decide in which register the following transactions will be recorded and analyze the transactions into their debit and credit parts. In Answers Column 1, print the abbreviation for the register in which each transaction is to be recorded. In Columns 2 and 3, print the letters identifying the accounts to be debited and credited for each transaction.

CR—check register **VR**—voucher register

Account Titles

A. Cash
B. Delivery Expense
C. Purchases
D. Purchases Discount
E. Vouchers Payable

Transactions	Answers 1 Reg.	2 Debit	3 Credit
1-2-3. Purchased merchandise on account. (p. 603)	1. ______	2. ______	3. ______
4-5-6. Received invoice for delivery expense. (p. 604)	4. ______	5. ______	6. ______
7-8-9. Paid voucher less a discount. (p. 606)	7. ______	8. ______	9. ______
10-11-12. Paid a voucher, no discount. (p. 606)	10. ______	11. ______	12. ______
13-14-15. Paid voucher for delivery expense. (p. 606)	13. ______	14. ______	15. ______

Part Three—Identifying Accounting Terms

Directions: Select the one term in Column I that best fits each definition in Column II. Print the letter identifying your choice in the Answers column. Note that there are more terms to choose from on the next page.

Column I

A. authority
B. check register
C. control activities
D. control environment
E. custody
F. error
G. financial statement misstatement
H. flowchart
I. fraud
J. information and communication
K. internal control structure
L. internal controls
M. invoice
N. monitoring

Column II	Answers
1. Processes and procedures employed within a business to ensure that its operations are conducted ethically, accurately, and reliably. (p. 592)	1. ______
2. An unintentional mistake. (p. 593)	2. ______
3. The theft of assets by employees or the intentional misstatement of financial information. (p. 593)	3. ______
4. The theft of assets by an employee. (p. 593)	4. ______
5. The manipulation of amounts reported on a financial statement. (p. 593)	5. ______
6. A process designed to achieve effectiveness and efficiency of operations, reliability of financial reporting, and compliance with applicable laws and regulations. (p. 593)	6. ______
7. The attitude and actions of management that indicate its commitment to strong internal controls and ethical standards. (p. 593)	7. ______
8. The process of determining whether an error or fraud could occur. (p. 593)	8. ______
9. The policies and procedures designed to prevent or detect errors or fraud. (p. 593)	9. ______

(continued on next page)

© 2020 Cengage®. May not be scanned, copied or duplicated, or posted to a publicly accessible website, in whole or in part.

Name ______________________________ Date ______________ Class ______________

Column I	Column II	Answers
O. narrative	**10.** The processes used to collect information about how the business is achieving its control goals. (p. 593)	**10.** ________
P. occupational fraud	**11.** The process management uses to determine whether its policies are operating effectively. (p. 593)	**11.** ________
Q. purchase order	**12.** Dividing the tasks of the accounting system among employees in different functions. (p. 594)	**12.** ________
R. receiving report	**13.** The ability of an employee to authorize a transaction. (p. 594)	**13.** ________
S. recording	**14.** The physical access to the assets involved in a transaction. (p. 594)	**14.** ________
T. requisition	**15.** The entry of a transaction in the financial records. (p. 594)	**15.** ________
U. risk assessment	**16.** A written description of the flow of documents and information between employees, departments, and external parties. (p. 597)	**16.** ________
V. segregation of duties	**17.** A diagram that uses symbols and connecting lines to represent a process. (p. 597)	**17.** ________
W. voucher	**18.** A collection of documents used to authorize a cash payment. (p. 601)	**18.** ________
X. voucher check	**19.** A set of procedures for controlling cash payments by preparing and approving vouchers before payments are made. (p. 601)	**19.** ________
Y. voucher register	**20.** A form requesting the purchase of merchandise. (p. 602)	**20.** ________
Z. voucher system	**21.** A form requesting that a vendor sell merchandise to a business. (p. 602)	**21.** ________
	22. A form that lists the item received from a vendor. (p. 602)	**22.** ________
	23. A form describing the goods or services sold, the quantity, the price, and the terms of sale. (p. 602)	**23.** ________
	24. A journal used to record vouchers. (p. 603)	**24.** ________
	25. A check with a detachable check stub, or voucher, that contains detailed information about the cash payment. (p. 605)	**25.** ________
	26. A journal used in a voucher system to record cash payments. (p. 606)	**26.** ________

© 2020 Cengage®. May not be scanned, copied or duplicated, or posted to a publicly accessible website, in whole or in part.

Name ______________________ Date ____________ Class ____________

20-1 WORK TOGETHER (LO3, 4), p. 596

Classify internal controls

1.

Item	Description	Component of the Internal Control Structure
1	A manager approves an employee's time card.	Control activities
2	A employee is able to call a hotline to report an ethics violation.	
3	Employees must sign a document stating that they will follow the guidance in the code of conduct.	
4	A monthly bank reconciliation is prepared for every bank account.	
5	Internal auditors regularly verify the authenticity of employees.	
6	An accountant considers how an employee could abuse a company credit card.	
7	A computer system prevents a salesclerk from changing the unit sales price of an item.	
8	Managers hold monthly meetings with employees to discuss problems and opportunities for improvement.	

2.

Item	Description	Function
1	A department store clerk processes a customer sale.	Authority
2	A clerk prepares checks based on documents approved by a manager.	
3	An accountant journalizes entries for depreciation.	
4	A warehouse clerk is responsible for high-priced items stored in a locked area of the warehouse.	
5	A sales manager approves the writing off of an uncollectible account.	
6	A manager signs off on the addition of a new company as an approved vendor.	
7	A sales representative has access to a company-owned tablet computer.	
8	An accountant journalizes the declaration of a dividend.	

© 2020 Cengage®. May not be scanned, copied or duplicated, or posted to a publicly accessible website, in whole or in part.

20-1 ON YOUR OWN (LO3, 4), p. 596

Classify internal controls

1.

Item	Description	Component of the Internal Control Structure
1	Management includes the phone number of the ethics officer in a weekly newsletter to emphasize that employees must follow the code of conduct.	
2	A payroll clerk verifies the mathematical accuracy of a time card.	
3	Accountants identify the amount of employee turnover in the Accounts Receivable Department.	
4	A security guard allows only employees and scheduled visitors into the office to prevent unauthorized access to accounting records.	
5	An internal auditor performs a test of payroll tax payments.	
6	A daily report of sales returns is submitted to the sales manager.	
7	The computer system does not allow a manager to enter a new employee.	
8	The company chief financial officer establishes a blog to answer employee questions regarding internal controls.	

2.

Item	Description	Function
1	A clerk deposits checks in the bank.	
2	A manager grants a sales allowance for damaged goods received by a customer.	
3	A warehouse clerk fills an order based on an approved form received from the Sales Department.	
4	An accountant enters a journal entry to correct a sale posted to the wrong customer account.	
5	A clerk maintains the petty cash fund.	
6	A salesclerk scans an item in a point-of-sale system.	
7	A payroll clerk enters the weekly hours worked by each employee.	
8	A sales representative submits a form instructing the company to ship merchandise to a customer.	

© 2020 Cengage®. May not be scanned, copied or duplicated, or posted to a publicly accessible website, in whole or in part.

Name ______________________ Date ____________ Class ____________

20-2 WORK TOGETHER (LO5), p. 600

Preparing flowcharts

a.

b.

© 2020 Cengage®. May not be scanned, copied or duplicated, or posted to a publicly accessible website, in whole or in part.

20-2 WORK TOGETHER (concluded)

c.

Warehouse Manager	Payroll Department

d.

Mailroom Clerk	Cashier

© 2020 Cengage®. May not be scanned, copied or duplicated, or posted to a publicly accessible website, in whole or in part.

Name ______________________ Date __________ Class __________

20-2 ON YOUR OWN (LO5), p. 600

Preparing flowcharts

a.

b.

© 2020 Cengage®. May not be scanned, copied or duplicated, or posted to a publicly accessible website, in whole or in part.

20-2 ON YOUR OWN (concluded)

c.

Credit Manager	Accounting Clerk

d.

Sales Representative	Salesclerk

© 2020 Cengage®. May not be scanned, copied or duplicated, or posted to a publicly accessible website, in whole or in part.

Name ______________________ Date ____________ Class ____________

20-3 WORK TOGETHER (LO6, 7), p. 607

Journalizing transactions in a voucher system

2., 3.

VOUCHER REGISTER

PAGE

	DATE	PAYEE	VCHR. NO.	PAID DATE	PAID CK. NO.	1 VOUCHERS PAYABLE CREDIT	2 PURCHASES DEBIT	3 SUPPLIES—SALES DEBIT	4 SUPPLIES—ADMIN. DEBIT	GENERAL ACCOUNT TITLE	GENERAL POST. REF.	5 GENERAL DEBIT	6 GENERAL CREDIT	
1														1
2														2
3														3
4														4
5														5
6														6

1., 2., 3.

CHECK REGISTER

PAGE

	DATE	PAYEE	CK. NO.	VCHR. NO.	1 VOUCHERS PAYABLE DEBIT	2 PURCHASES DISCOUNT CREDIT	3 CASH CREDIT	4 BANK DEPOSITS	5 BANK BALANCE	
1										1
2										2
3										3
4										4
5										5
6										6
7										7
8										8

© 2020 Cengage®. May not be scanned, copied or duplicated, or posted to a publicly accessible website, in whole or in part.

20-3 ON YOUR OWN (LO6, 7), p. 607

Journalizing transactions in a voucher system

2., 3.

VOUCHER REGISTER

PAGE

	DATE	PAYEE	VCHR. NO.	PAID DATE	PAID CK. NO.	1 VOUCHERS PAYABLE CREDIT	2 PURCHASES DEBIT	3 SUPPLIES—SALES DEBIT	4 SUPPLIES—ADMIN. DEBIT	GENERAL ACCOUNT TITLE	GENERAL POST. REF.	5 GENERAL DEBIT	6 GENERAL CREDIT	
1														1
2														2
3														3
4														4
5														5
6														6

1., 2., 3.

CHECK REGISTER

PAGE

	DATE	PAYEE	CK. NO.	VCHR. NO.	1 VOUCHERS PAYABLE DEBIT	2 PURCHASES DISCOUNT CREDIT	3 CASH CREDIT	4 BANK DEPOSITS	5 BANK BALANCE	
1										1
2										2
3										3
4										4
5										5
6										6
7										7
8										8

© 2020 Cengage®. May not be scanned, copied or duplicated, or posted to a publicly accessible website, in whole or in part.

Name ______________________ Date ____________ Class ____________

20-4 WORK TOGETHER (LO8), p. 611

Performing a risk assessment

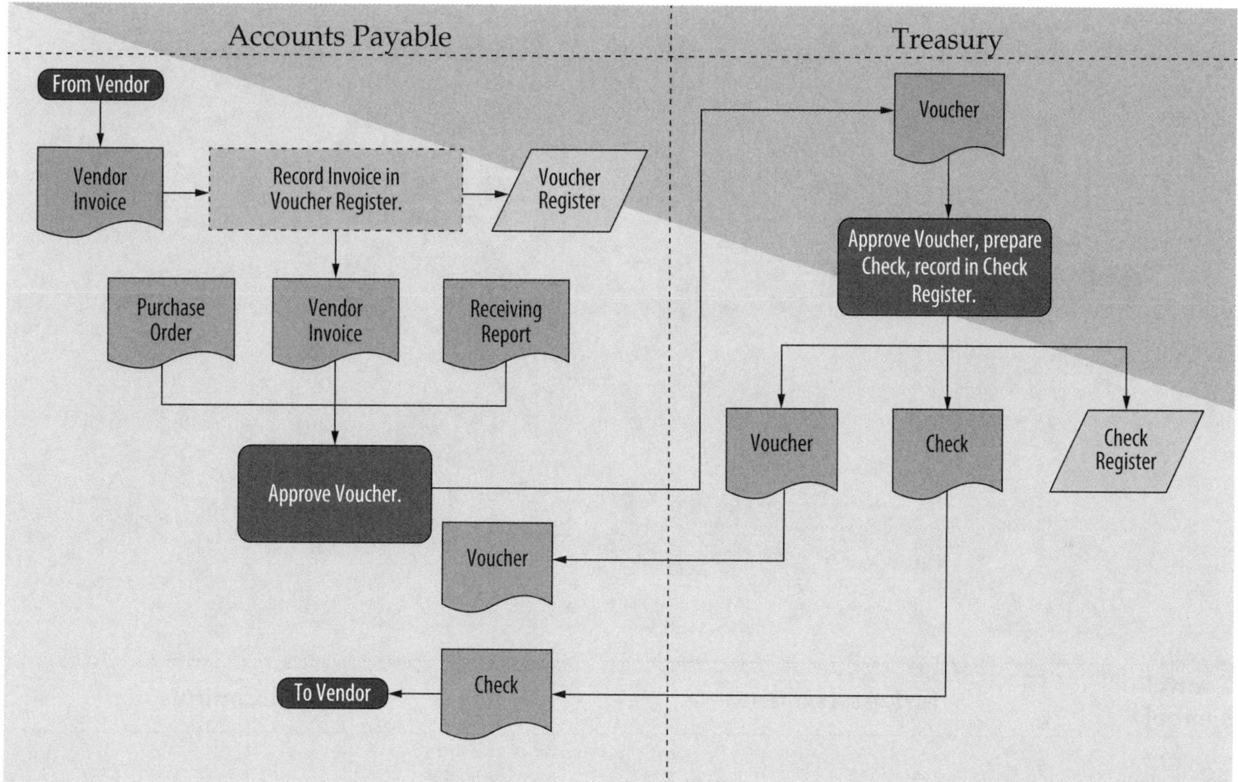

Control Symbol	Risk Assessment	Internal Control
①		
②		
③		

© 2020 Cengage®. May not be scanned, copied or duplicated, or posted to a publicly accessible website, in whole or in part.

20-4 ON YOUR OWN (LO8), p. 611

Performing a risk assessment

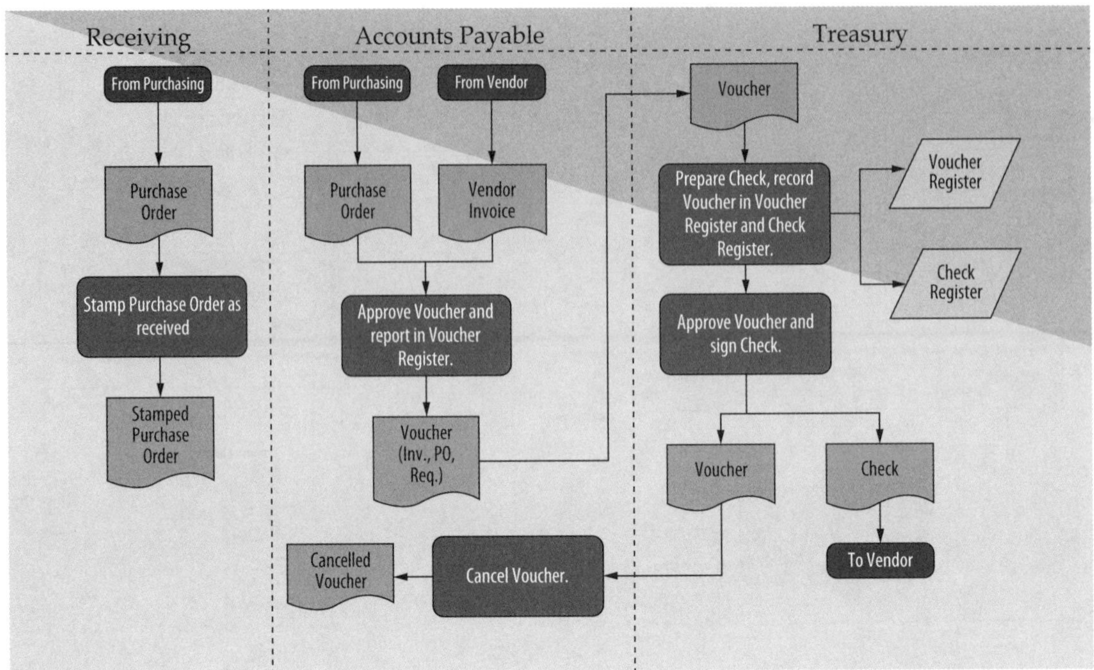

Control Symbol	Risk Assessment	Internal Control
①		
②		
③		
④		

© 2020 Cengage®. May not be scanned, copied or duplicated, or posted to a publicly accessible website, in whole or in part.

Name ______________________ Date ____________ Class ____________

20-1 APPLICATION PROBLEM (LO3, 4), p. 615

Classify internal controls

1.

Item	Description	Component of the Internal Control Structure
1	A manager approves a sales return.	
2	An employee compares a schedule of accounts receivable to the general ledger balance of a controlling account.	
3	A report is sent to the technology officer showing the number of times an unauthorized person attempted to access the computer system.	
4	Employees are required to pass an online quiz assessing their knowledge of customer confidentiality policies.	
5	Employees are encouraged to report questionable transactions to the ethics officer of a business.	
6	An accountant considers how a cashier could take money from the cash register without being detected.	
7	The computer system does not allow a purchasing clerk to enter a new vendor without authorization by the purchasing manager.	
8	Internal auditors examine the voucher documentation for a group of checks.	

2.

Item	Description	Function
1	A shipping clerk receives merchandise from the warehouse.	
2	An accountant records a journal entry to adjust a prepaid expense account.	
3	A restaurant employee takes a customer's order.	
4	A warehouse clerk enters information in the computer system to write off damaged merchandise.	
5	A manager prepares a requisition for the purchase of new computer equipment.	
6	A sales representative is assigned a car to travel to visit customers.	
7	A credit manager approves a credit limit for a customer.	
8	A manager approves the reduction of unit sales prices.	

© 2020 Cengage®. May not be scanned, copied or duplicated, or posted to a publicly accessible website, in whole or in part.

20-2 APPLICATION PROBLEM (LO5), p. 615

Preparing flowcharts

a.

b.

© 2020 Cengage®. May not be scanned, copied or duplicated, or posted to a publicly accessible website, in whole or in part.

Name ______________________ Date ____________ Class ____________

20-2 APPLICATION PROBLEM (concluded)

c.

Warehouse Employee	Shipping Department

d.

Receptionist	Accounting Clerk

© 2020 Cengage®. May not be scanned, copied or duplicated, or posted to a publicly accessible website, in whole or in part.

20-3 APPLICATION PROBLEM (LO6, 7), p. 615

Journalizing transactions in a voucher system

2., 3.

VOUCHER REGISTER

PAGE

	DATE	PAYEE	VCHR. NO.	PAID DATE	PAID CK. NO.	1 VOUCHERS PAYABLE CREDIT	2 PURCHASES DEBIT	3 SUPPLIES—SALES DEBIT	4 SUPPLIES—ADMIN. DEBIT	GENERAL ACCOUNT TITLE	GENERAL POST. REF.	5 GENERAL DEBIT	6 GENERAL CREDIT	
1														1
2														2
3														3
4														4
5														5
6														6

1., 2., 4.

CHECK REGISTER

PAGE

	DATE	PAYEE	CK. NO.	VCHR. NO.	1 VOUCHERS PAYABLE DEBIT	2 PURCHASES DISCOUNT CREDIT	3 CASH CREDIT	4 BANK DEPOSITS	5 BANK BALANCE	
1										1
2										2
3										3
4										4
5										5
6										6
7										7
8										8

© 2020 Cengage®. May not be scanned, copied or duplicated, or posted to a publicly accessible website, in whole or in part.

Name ______________________ Date ____________ Class ____________

20-4 APPLICATION PROBLEM (LO8), p. 616

Performing a risk assessment

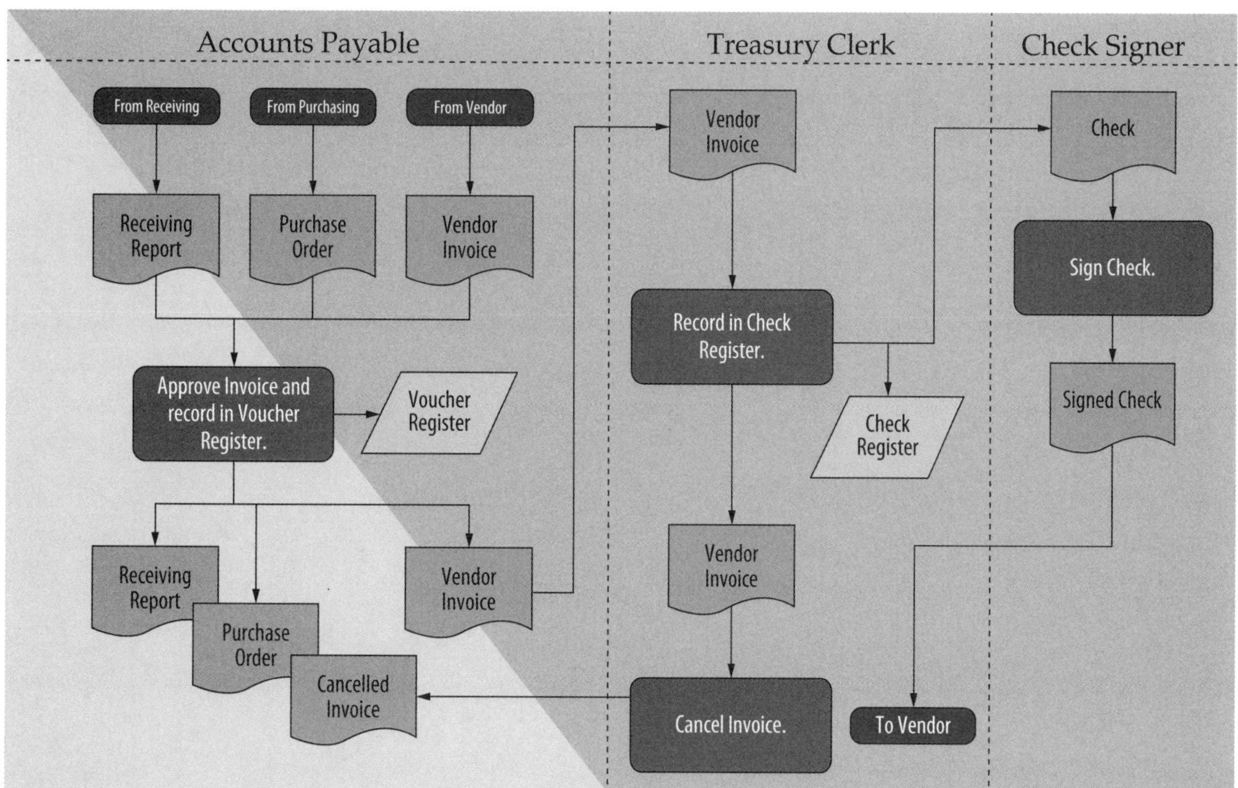

Control Symbol	Risk Assessment	Internal Control
①		
②		
③		
④		

© 2020 Cengage®. May not be scanned, copied or duplicated, or posted to a publicly accessible website, in whole or in part.

20-M MASTERY PROBLEM (LO5, 6, 7, 8), p. 616

Analyzing a voucher system and journalizing transactions in a voucher system

1.

© 2020 Cengage®. May not be scanned, copied or duplicated, or posted to a publicly accessible website, in whole or in part.

Name ______________________ Date ____________ Class ____________

20-M MASTERY PROBLEM (continued)

2.

Control Symbol	Risk Assessment	Internal Control
①		
②		
③		
④		

© 2020 Cengage®. May not be scanned, copied or duplicated, or posted to a publicly accessible website, in whole or in part.

20-M MASTERY PROBLEM (concluded)

Analyzing a voucher system and journalizing transactions in a voucher system

3., 4., 5.

VOUCHER REGISTER

PAGE

	DATE		PAYEE	VCHR. NO.	PAID DATE	PAID CK. NO.	1 VOUCHERS PAYABLE CREDIT	2 PURCHASES DEBIT	3 SUPPLIES—SALES DEBIT	4 SUPPLIES—ADMIN. DEBIT	GENERAL ACCOUNT TITLE	GENERAL POST. REF.	5 GENERAL DEBIT	6 GENERAL CREDIT	
1	20– Aug.														1
2															2
3															3
4															4
5															5
6															6

3., 4., 5.

CHECK REGISTER

PAGE

	DATE		PAYEE	CK. NO.	VCHR. NO.	1 VOUCHERS PAYABLE DEBIT	2 PURCHASES DISCOUNT CREDIT	3 CASH CREDIT	4 BANK DEPOSITS	5 BANK BALANCE	
1	20– Aug.	1	Balance Forward							9 418 25	1
2											2
3											3
4											4
5											5
6											6
7											7
8											8

© 2020 Cengage®. May not be scanned, copied or duplicated, or posted to a publicly accessible website, in whole or in part.

Name ______________________ Date ______________ Class ______________

20-C CHALLENGE PROBLEM (LO5, 8), p. 617

Completing a flowchart

Symbol	Description
A	From customer
B	
C	
D	
E	
F	
G	

© 2020 Cengage®. May not be scanned, copied or duplicated, or posted to a publicly accessible website, in whole or in part.

Name	Perfect Score	Your Score
Analyzing Concepts for the Organizational Structure of Partnerships	15 Pts.	
Analyzing Partnerships Equity Transactions	12 Pts.	
Analyzing Transactions for Admitting a New Partner	8 Pts.	
Total	35 Pts.	

Part One—Analyzing Concepts for the Organizational Structure of Partnerships

Directions: Place a *T* for True or an *F* for False in the Answers column to show whether each of the following statements is true or false.

	Answers
1. The partners' ownership is recorded in an equity account for each partner. (p. 623)	**1.** ______
2. A partnership has an unlimited life, unlike a sole proprietorship, which has a limited life. (p. 623)	**2.** ______
3. A partnership is created when two or more persons agree orally or in writing to start a business, using the partnership form of organization. (p. 624)	**3.** ______
4. Unlike other forms of business, a partnership's financial records are kept separate from those of the partners. (p. 624)	**4.** ______
5. The Internal Revenue Service considers the money that partners receive from a partnership to be salaries. (p. 624)	**5.** ______
6. A written agreement setting forth the conditions under which a partnership is to operate is called a partnership agreement. (p. 624)	**6.** ______
7. The right of all partners to contract for a partnership is called mutual agency. (p. 624)	**7.** ______
8. A partnership agreement may be prepared in writing. (p. 624)	**8.** ______
9. A financial statement that presents the fair market value of a company's assets, liabilities, and owner's equity is called a balance sheet. (p. 627)	**9.** ______
10. The value of a business can be determined based on the amount of revenue the business can generate. (p. 633)	**10.** ______
11. The value of the assets of a professional services business is relatively small compared to the fees that the business can earn. (p. 633)	**11.** ______
12. The total investment of owners in excess of the value of a business is called goodwill. (p. 633)	**12.** ______
13. Two journal entries are required when a partner is admitted to a partnership and goodwill is recognized. (p. 633)	**13.** ______
14. An ongoing business may be worth more than the equity value stated in the accounting records. (p. 634)	**14.** ______
15. The account Goodwill is located in a general ledger's Intangible Liabilities section. (p. 634)	**15.** ______

© 2020 Cengage®. May not be scanned, copied or duplicated, or posted to a publicly accessible website, in whole or in part.

Part Two—Analyzing Partnerships Equity Transactions

Directions: Ross Adams and Saul Best are partners in an existing partnership and share equally in all distributions. For each of the following independent transactions, print in the proper Answers column the identifying letters of the accounts to be debited and credited.

Account Titles

A. Accounts Payable
B. Cash
C. Inventory
D. Goodwill
E. Ross Adams, Capital
F. Saul Best, Capital
G. Tasha Clay, Capital

Transactions	Answers Debit	Answers Credit
1-2. Received cash from partner, Ross Adams, as an initial investment. (p. 628)	1.______	2.______
3-4. Accepted the cash, inventory, and accounts payable of Saul Best's existing business as an initial investment. (p. 628)	3.______	4.______
5-6. Ross Adams and Saul Best sold equity to a new partner, Tasha Clay, for a one-third equity in the partnership. Ross and Saul receive cash from Tasha for their partnership equity. (p. 630)	5.______	6.______
7-8. The partnership received cash from new partner, Tasha Clay, for a one-third equity in the partnership. Tasha paid an amount equal to the capital account balances of each partner. (p. 631)	7.______	8.______
9-10. Received cash from new partner, Tasha Clay, for a one-third equity in the partnership. Tasha paid an amount less than the capital account balances of each partner. Existing equity is redistributed between the existing partners, Ross Adams and Saul Best. (p. 632)	9.______	10.______
11-12. Received cash from new partner, Tasha Clay, for a one-third equity in the partnership. Tasha believes the value of the business is greater than the existing partners' investments. (p. 633)	11.______	12.______

© 2020 Cengage®. May not be scanned, copied or duplicated, or posted to a publicly accessible website, in whole or in part.

Name ________________________ Date ____________ Class ____________

Part Three—Analyzing Transactions for Admitting a New Partner

Directions: Ross Adams and Saul Best each have $30,000 of equity in their partnership and share equally in all distributions. For each of the following independent transactions, select the choice that best completes the sentence. Print the letter identifying your choice in the Answers column.

Answers

1. Ross Adams and Saul Best personally sell Tasha Clay a one-third equity in the partnership. Ross and Saul receive cash from Tasha for their partnership equity. The transaction would include a debit to Ross Adams, Capital, for (p. 630) **1.** ______

a. $5,000 **c.** $10,000
b. $15,000 **d.** $20,000

2. Ross Adams and Saul Best personally sell Tasha Clay a one-fourth equity in the partnership. Ross and Saul receive cash from Tasha for their partnership equity. Tasha paid each of the partners (p. 630) **2.** ______

a. $5,000 **c.** $10,000
b. $7,500 **d.** $12,500

3. The partnership received $30,000 cash from new partner, Tasha Clay, for a one-third equity in the partnership. The transaction would include a debit to Ross Adams, Capital, for (p. 631) **3.** ______

a. $0 **c.** $10,000
b. $5,000 **d.** $15,000

4. The partnership received cash from new partner, Tasha Clay, for a one-fourth equity in the partnership. Tasha paid the partnership (p. 631) **4.** ______

a. $15,000 **c.** $25,000
b. $20,000 **d.** $30,000

5. The partnership received $24,000 cash from new partner, Tasha Clay, for a one-third equity in the partnership. The transaction would include a debit to Ross Adams, Capital, for (p. 632) **5.** ______

a. $0 **c.** $3,000
b. $2,000 **d.** $5,000

6. The partnership received $18,000 cash from new partner, Tasha Clay, for a one-fourth equity in the partnership. After recording the transaction, Tasha Clay's capital account will have a balance of (p. 632) **6.** ______

a. $18,000 **c.** $19,000
b. $18,500 **d.** $19,500

7. Received $40,000 cash from new partner, Tasha Clay, for a one-third equity in the business. The transaction would include a debit to Goodwill for (p. 633) **7.** ______

a. $0 **c.** $20,000
b. $10,000 **d.** $30,000

8. Received $40,000 cash from new partner, Tasha Clay, for a one-third equity in the business. The transaction would include a credit to Ross Adams, Capital, for (p. 633) **8.** ______

a. $0 **c.** $7,500
b. $5,000 **d.** $10,000

© 2020 Cengage®. May not be scanned, copied or duplicated, or posted to a publicly accessible website, in whole or in part.

Name ______________________ Date ____________ Class ____________

21-1 WORK TOGETHER, p. 629

Forming a partnership

CASH RECEIPTS JOURNAL

PAGE 1

	DATE	ACCOUNT TITLE	DOC. NO.	POST. REF.	1 GENERAL DEBIT	2 GENERAL CREDIT	3 ACCOUNTS RECEIVABLE CREDIT	4 SALES CREDIT	5 SALES TAX PAYABLE CREDIT	6 SALES DISCOUNT DEBIT	7 CASH DEBIT	
1												1
2												2
3												3
4												4
5												5
6												6
7												7
8												8
9												9
10												10
11												11
12												12
13												13
14												14
15												15
16												16
17												17
18												18
19												19
20												20
21												21
22												22

© 2020 Cengage®. May not be scanned, copied or duplicated, or posted to a publicly accessible website, in whole or in part.

Milner Cycle Shop

Fair Market Value Balance Sheet

May 1, 20--

ASSETS			
Current Assets:			
Cash		2,058.50	
Accounts Receivable	8,156.15		
Less Allowance for Uncollectible Accounts	400.00	7,756.15	
Inventory		42,060.00	
Supplies		780.00	
Total Current Assets			52,654.65
Plant Assets:			
Equipment			16,500.00
Total Assets			69,154.65
LIABILITIES			
Accounts Payable			9,154.65
OWNER'S EQUITY			
Keel Milner, Capital			60,000.00
Total Laibilities and Owner's Equity			69,154.65

© 2020 Cengage®. May not be scanned, copied or duplicated, or posted to a publicly accessible website, in whole or in part.

Name ______________________ Date ____________ Class ____________

21-1 ON YOUR OWN, p. 629

CASH RECEIPTS JOURNAL

PAGE 1

				1	2	3	4	5	6	7	
				GENERAL							
	DATE	ACCOUNT TITLE	DOC. NO.	POST. REF.	DEBIT	CREDIT	ACCOUNTS RECEIVABLE CREDIT	SALES CREDIT	SALES TAX PAYABLE CREDIT	SALES DISCOUNT DEBIT	CASH DEBIT
1											1
2											2
3											3
4											4
5											5
6											6
7											7
8											8
9											9
10											10
11											11
12											12
13											13
14											14
15											15
16											16
17											17
18											18
19											19
20											20
21											21
22											22

Forming a partnership

© 2020 Cengage®. May not be scanned, copied or duplicated, or posted to a publicly accessible website, in whole or in part.

Stapp Carpet Center

Fair Market Value Balance Sheet

July 1, 20--

ASSETS			
Current Assets:			
Cash		7,856.04	
Accounts Receivable	6,148.62		
Less Allowance for Uncollectible Accounts	250.00	5,898.62	
Inventory		14,850.00	
Supplies		1,080.00	
Total Current Assets			29,684.66
Plant Assets:			
Equipment			14,500.00
Total Assets			44,184.66
LIABILITIES			
Accounts Payable			6,184.66
OWNER'S EQUITY			
Janey Stapp, Capital			38,000.00
Total Laibilities and Owner's Equity			44,184.66

© 2020 Cengage®. May not be scanned, copied or duplicated, or posted to a publicly accessible website, in whole or in part.

Name ______________________ Date ____________ Class ____________

21-2 WORK TOGETHER, p. 636

Admitting partners to existing partnerships

GENERAL JOURNAL PAGE 4

		DATE		ACCOUNT TITLE	DOC. NO.	POST. REF.	DEBIT	CREDIT	
1.	1								1
	2								2
	3								3
	4								4
	5								5
	6								6
3.	7								7
	8								8
	9								9
	10								10
	11								11
	12								12
4.	13								13
	14								14
	15								15
	16								16
	17								17
	18								18
	19								19
	20								20
	21								21
	22								22
	23								23
	24								24
	25								25
	26								26
	27								27
	28								28
	29								29
	30								30
	31								31
	32								32

© 2020 Cengage®. May not be scanned, copied or duplicated, or posted to a publicly accessible website, in whole or in part.

21-2 WORK TOGETHER (concluded)

CASH RECEIPTS JOURNAL

PAGE 14

					1	2	3	4	5	6	7	
	DATE	ACCOUNT TITLE	DOC. NO.	POST. REF.	GENERAL DEBIT	GENERAL CREDIT	ACCOUNTS RECEIVABLE CREDIT	SALES CREDIT	SALES TAX PAYABLE CREDIT	SALES DISCOUNT DEBIT	CASH DEBIT	
1												1
2												2
3												3
4												4
5												5
6												6
7												7
8												8
9												9
10												10
11												11
12												12
13												13
14												14
15												15
16												16
17												17
18												18
19												19
20												20
21												21
22												22

2. **3.** **4.**

© 2020 Cengage®. May not be scanned, copied or duplicated, or posted to a publicly accessible website, in whole or in part.

Name ______________________ Date ______________ Class ______________

21-2 ON YOUR OWN, p. 636

Admitting partners to existing partnerships

GENERAL JOURNAL PAGE 7

		DATE	ACCOUNT TITLE	DOC. NO.	POST. REF.	DEBIT	CREDIT	
1.	1							1
	2							2
	3							3
	4							4
	5							5
	6							6
3.	7							7
	8							8
	9							9
	10							10
	11							11
	12							12
4.	13							13
	14							14
	15							15
	16							16
	17							17
	18							18
	19							19
	20							20
	21							21
	22							22
	23							23
	24							24
	25							25
	26							26
	27							27
	28							28
	29							29
	30							30
	31							31
	32							32

© 2020 Cengage®. May not be scanned, copied or duplicated, or posted to a publicly accessible website, in whole or in part.

CASH RECEIPTS JOURNAL

PAGE 12

		DATE	ACCOUNT TITLE	DOC. NO.	POST. REF.	1 GENERAL DEBIT	2 GENERAL CREDIT	3 ACCOUNTS RECEIVABLE CREDIT	4 SALES CREDIT	5 SALES TAX PAYABLE CREDIT	6 SALES DISCOUNT DEBIT	7 CASH DEBIT	
2.	1												1
	2												2
	3												3
3.	4												4
	5												5
	6												6
4.	7												7
	8												8
	9												9
	10												10
	11												11
	12												12
	13												13
	14												14
	15												15
	16												16
	17												17
	18												18
	19												19
	20												20
	21												21
	22												22

© 2020 Cengage®. May not be scanned, copied or duplicated, or posted to a publicly accessible website, in whole or in part.

Name ____________________ Date ____________ Class ____________

21-1 APPLICATION PROBLEM (LO2), p. 638

Forming a partnership

CASH RECEIPTS JOURNAL

PAGE 1

	DATE	ACCOUNT TITLE	DOC. NO.	POST. REF.	1 GENERAL DEBIT	2 GENERAL CREDIT	3 ACCOUNTS RECEIVABLE CREDIT	4 SALES CREDIT	5 SALES TAX PAYABLE CREDIT	6 SALES DISCOUNT DEBIT	7 CASH DEBIT	
1												1
2												2
3												3
4												4
5												5
6												6
7												7
8												8
9												9
10												10
11												11
12												12
13												13
14												14
15												15
16												16
17												17
18												18
19												19
20												20
21												21
22												22

© 2020 Cengage®. May not be scanned, copied or duplicated, or posted to a publicly accessible website, in whole or in part.

21-2 APPLICATION PROBLEM (LO3), p. 639

Admitting a partner with no change in total equity

GENERAL JOURNAL PAGE 4

		DATE		ACCOUNT TITLE	DOC. NO.	POST. REF.	DEBIT	CREDIT	
1.	1								1
	2								2
	3								3
	4								4
	5								5
	6								6
3.	7								7
	8								8
	9								9
	10								10
	11								11
	12								12
4.	13								13
	14								14
	15								15
	16								16
	17								17
	18								18
	19								19
	20								20
	21								21
	22								22
	23								23
	24								24
	25								25
	26								26
	27								27
	28								28
	29								29
	30								30
	31								31
	32								32

© 2020 Cengage®. May not be scanned, copied or duplicated, or posted to a publicly accessible website, in whole or in part.

Name ______________________ Date ____________ Class ____________

21-2 APPLICATION PROBLEM (concluded)

CASH RECEIPTS JOURNAL

PAGE 7

DATE	ACCOUNT TITLE	DOC. NO.	POST. REF.	1 GENERAL DEBIT	2 GENERAL CREDIT	3 ACCOUNTS RECEIVABLE CREDIT	4 SALES CREDIT	5 SALES TAX PAYABLE CREDIT	6 SALES DISCOUNT DEBIT	7 CASH DEBIT

2.

3.

4.

© 2020 Cengage®. May not be scanned, copied or duplicated, or posted to a publicly accessible website, in whole or in part.

21-M MASTERY PROBLEM (LO2, 3), p. 640

Forming and expanding a partnership

GENERAL JOURNAL PAGE 1

DATE		ACCOUNT TITLE	DOC. NO.	POST. REF.	DEBIT	CREDIT

© 2020 Cengage®. May not be scanned, copied or duplicated, or posted to a publicly accessible website, in whole or in part.

Name ______________________ Date ____________ Class ____________

21-M MASTERY PROBLEM (concluded)

CASH RECEIPTS JOURNAL PAGE 1

	DATE	ACCOUNT TITLE	DOC. NO.	POST. REF.	1 GENERAL DEBIT	2 GENERAL CREDIT	3 ACCOUNTS RECEIVABLE CREDIT	4 SALES CREDIT	5 SALES TAX PAYABLE CREDIT	6 SALES DISCOUNT DEBIT	7 CASH DEBIT	
1												1
2												2
3												3
4												4
5												5
6												6
7												7
8												8
9												9
10												10
11												11
12												12
13												13
14												14
15												15
16												16
17												17
18												18
19												19
20												20
21												21
22												22

© 2020 Cengage®. May not be scanned, copied or duplicated, or posted to a publicly accessible website, in whole or in part.

21-C CHALLENGE PROBLEM (LO2, 3), p. 641

Expanding a partnership

GENERAL JOURNAL PAGE 3

	DATE		ACCOUNT TITLE	DOC. NO.	POST. REF.	DEBIT	CREDIT	
1								1
2								2
3								3
4								4
5								5
6								6
7								7
8								8
9								9
10								10
11								11
12								12
13								13
14								14
15								15
16								16
17								17
18								18
19								19
20								20
21								21
22								22
23								23
24								24
25								25
26								26
27								27
28								28
29								29
30								30
31								31
32								32

© 2020 Cengage®. May not be scanned, copied or duplicated, or posted to a publicly accessible website, in whole or in part.

Name ______________________ Date ____________ Class ____________

21-C CHALLENGE PROBLEM (continued)

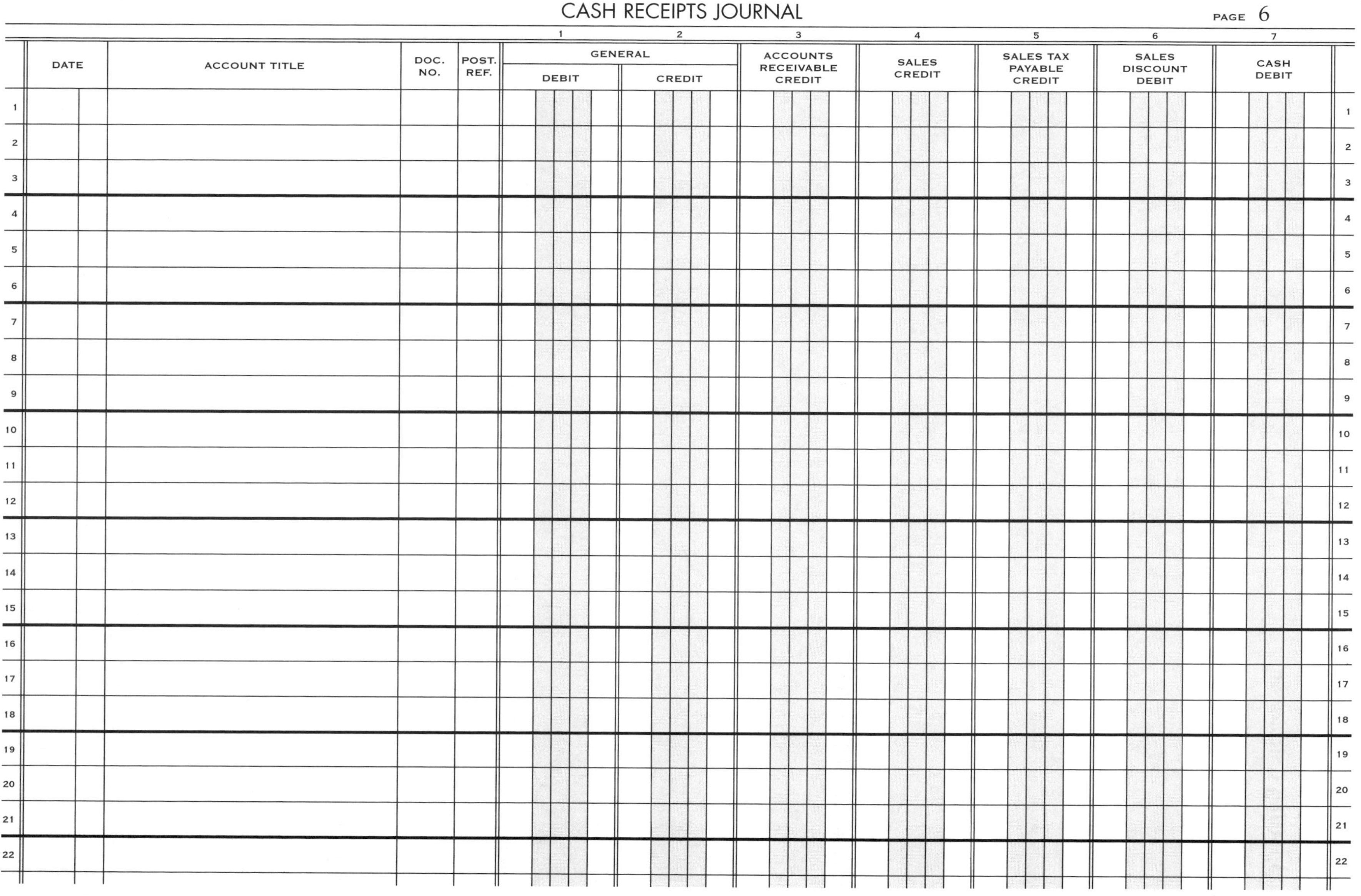

CASH RECEIPTS JOURNAL PAGE 6

	DATE	ACCOUNT TITLE	DOC. NO.	POST. REF.	1 GENERAL DEBIT	2 GENERAL CREDIT	3 ACCOUNTS RECEIVABLE CREDIT	4 SALES CREDIT	5 SALES TAX PAYABLE CREDIT	6 SALES DISCOUNT DEBIT	7 CASH DEBIT	
1												1
2												2
3												3
4												4
5												5
6												6
7												7
8												8
9												9
10												10
11												11
12												12
13												13
14												14
15												15
16												16
17												17
18												18
19												19
20												20
21												21
22												22

© 2020 Cengage®. May not be scanned, copied or duplicated, or posted to a publicly accessible website, in whole or in part.

21-C CHALLENGE PROBLEM (continued)

Supporting Calculations

Mar. 9

Calculation of Total Recorded Equity and Allocation of Goodwill

Aug. 14

© 2020 Cengage®. May not be scanned, copied or duplicated, or posted to a publicly accessible website, in whole or in part.

Name ______________________ Date ____________ Class ____________

21-C CHALLENGE PROBLEM (concluded)

Dec. 9

Calculation of Total Recorded Equity and Allocation of Goodwill

© 2020 Cengage®. May not be scanned, copied or duplicated, or posted to a publicly accessible website, in whole or in part.

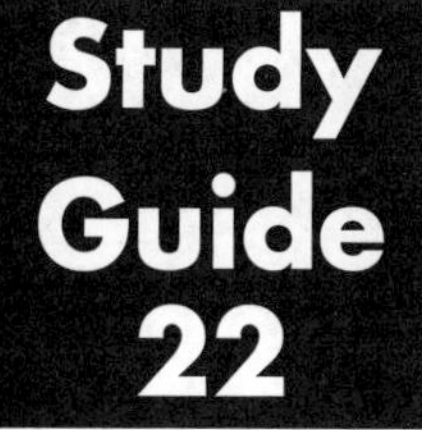

Name		Perfect Score	Your Score
	Analyzing Concepts for Financial Reporting for a Partnership	20 Pts.	
	Analyzing Partnership Transactions	20 Pts.	
	Calculating Distribution of Net Income, Net Loss, or Distribution Deficit	12 Pts.	
	Total	52 Pts.	

Part One—Analyzing Concepts for Financial Reporting for a Partnership

Directions: Place a *T* for True or an *F* for False in the Answers column to show whether each of the following statements is true or false.

Answers

1. If a partnership agreement includes nothing about how earnings are to be distributed, the partners usually share according to a fixed percentage of 50% and 50%. (p. 647) **1.** ______
2. Salaries are often paid to partners who devote time to working for the partnership. (p. 648) **2.** ______
3. When salaries or interest on equity are allowed, the amounts allowed are credited to partners' capital only if there is sufficient net income. (p. 650) **3.** ______
4. The amount by which distributions to partners exceed net income is called a distribution deficit. (p. 650) **4.** ______
5. Partners may take assets out of a partnership during a fiscal year in anticipation of the net income for the year. (p. 650) **5.** ______
6. If a partner takes inventory out of a partnership for personal use, it is an expense of the partnership. (p. 650) **6.** ______
7. Partnerships pay federal income taxes on all net income earned by the partnership. (p. 653) **7.** ______
8. A partnership owners' equity statement serves the same purpose as a corporate statement of stockholders' equity. (p. 654) **8.** ______
9. The major difference between a partnership balance sheet and a corporate balance sheet is how the owners' equity is reported. (p. 655) **9.** ______
10. The Internal Revenue Service considers partners who draw salaries to be employees of the partnership. (p. 656) **10.** ______
11. A partnership submits a Form 1065 to the Internal Revenue Service, showing the amount of earnings distributed to each partner. (p. 656) **11.** ______
12. The partners deduct the amount of cash and assets taken out of the partnership on their personal income tax returns. (p. 656) **12.** ______
13. A partners' self-employment tax rate is the same as that of an employed individual's social security and Medicare tax rates. (p. 656) **13.** ______
14. Not recording partners' self-employment taxes on partnership records is an application of the accounting concept, Business Entity. (p. 656) **14.** ______
15. The process of paying a partnership's liabilities and distributing remaining assets to the partners is called termination of a partnership. (p. 658) **15.** ______
16. Cash received from the sale of assets during liquidation of a partnership is called realization. (p. 658) **16.** ______
17. When an asset is sold for less than the recorded book value, the loss is recorded in the account Realization Expense. (p. 659) **17.** ______

© 2020 Cengage®. May not be scanned, copied or duplicated, or posted to a publicly accessible website, in whole or in part.

Answers

18. Liquidating liabilities typically results in a gain or loss on liquidation. (p. 661) 18. ______

19. When all creditors have been paid, the balance of Gain or Loss on Realization is distributed to the partners. (p. 662) 19. ______

20. A credit balance in the account Gain or Loss on Realization indicates a gain on realization. (p. 662) 20. ______

Part Two—Analyzing Partnership Transactions

Directions: For each transaction below, print in the proper Answers columns the identifying letter of the accounts to be debited and credited.

Account Titles

A. Cash
B. Gain or Loss on Realization
C. Income Summary
D. Partner A, Capital
E. Partner A, Drawing
F. Partner B, Capital
G. Partner B, Drawing
H. Supplies

Transactions	Answers Debit	Answers Credit
1-2. Partner A withdrew cash for personal use. (p. 650)	1. ______	2. ______
3-4. Partner B took supplies for personal use. (p. 651)	3. ______	4. ______
5-6. Journal entry to record Partner A's share of net income. (p. 655)	5. ______	6. ______
7-8. Journal entry to record Partner B's share of net income. (p. 655)	7. ______	8. ______
9-10. Journal entry to close Partner A's drawing account. (p. 655)	9. ______	10. ______
11-12. Journal entry to close Partner B's drawing account. (p. 655)	11. ______	12. ______
13-14. Journal entry to record sale of supplies for more than book value during liquidation. (p. 658)	13. ______	14. ______
15-16. Journal entry to record sale of supplies for less than book value during liquidation. (p. 659)	15. ______	16. ______
17-18. Journal entry to distribute credit balance of Gain or Loss on Realization to Partners A and B during liquidation. (p. 662)	17. ______	18. ______
19-20. Journal entry to record distribution of remaining cash to Partners A and B during final liquidation. (p. 662)	19. ______	20. ______

© 2020 Cengage®. May not be scanned, copied or duplicated, or posted to a publicly accessible website, in whole or in part.

Name ______________________ Date ______________ Class ______________

Part Three—Calculating Distribution of Net Income, Net Loss, or Distribution Deficit

Directions: Calculate each partner's share of the net income in each situation below. Write the amounts due each partner in the Answers columns. Beginning equity is: Partner A, $30,000.00; Partner B, $20,000.00. Net income for the fiscal year is $15,000.00.

	Answers	
	Partner A	**Partner B**
1-2. Using fixed percentage of 50% and 50%. (p. 647)	**1.** ________	**2.** ________
3-4. Using a percentage of each partner's equity to total equity. (p. 647)	**3.** ________	**4.** ________
5-6. Using interest on equity of 12% and dividing the remainder equally. (p. 648)	**5.** ________	**6.** ________
7-8. Using partners' salaries: Partner A, $6,000.00; Partner B, $5,000.00; dividing the remainder equally. (p. 648)	**7.** ________	**8.** ________
9-10. Using interest on equity of 8%, salary of $5,000.00 to each partner, and dividing the remainder equally. (p. 649)	**9.** ________	**10.** ________
11-12. Using interest on equity of 10%, salary of $8,000.00 to Partner A and $10,000.00 to Partner B, and dividing the remainder equally. (p. 650)	**11.** ________	**12.** ________

© 2020 Cengage®. May not be scanned, copied or duplicated, or posted to a publicly accessible website, in whole or in part.

Name ______________________ Date ____________ Class ____________

22-1 WORK TOGETHER (LO1, 2), p. 652

Calculating partnership earnings and journalizing partnership withdrawals

1. a. Percentage of total equity

	Partner's Equity	÷	Total Equity	=	Percentage of Total Equity
Jen Turner					
Lavenia Hogan					
Total equity					

	Total Net Income	×	Percentage of Total Equity	=	Share of Net Income
Jen Turner					
Lavenia Hogan					
Total net income					

1. b. Interest on equity plus fixed percentage

	Partner's Equity	×	Interest Rate	=	Interest on Equity
Jen Turner					
Lavenia Hogan					
Total interest					

Net Income	–	Total Interest	=	Remaining Net Income

	Remaining Net Income	×	Fixed Percentage	=	Partner's Share
Jen Turner					
Lavenia Hogan					
Total remaining net income					

	Interest on Equity	+	Remaining Net Income	=	Partner's Share
Jen Turner					
Lavenia Hogan					
Total net income					

© 2020 Cengage®. May not be scanned, copied or duplicated, or posted to a publicly accessible website, in whole or in part.

22-1 WORK TOGETHER (continued)

2.

	Partner's Equity	×	Interest Rate	=	Interest on Equity
Jen Turner					
Lavenia Hogan					
Total interest					

Net Income	–	Total Interest	–	Total Salaries	=	Distribution Deficit

	Distribution Deficit	×	Fixed Percentage	=	Partner's Share
Jen Turner					
Lavenia Hogan					
Total distribution deficit					

	Interest on Equity	+	Salary	+	Distribution Deficit	=	Partner's Total Share
Jen Turner							
Lavenia Hogan							
Total net income							

3.

GENERAL JOURNAL PAGE 9

	DATE		ACCOUNT TITLE	DOC. NO.	POST. REF.	DEBIT	CREDIT	
1								1
2								2
3								3
4								4
5								5
6								6
7								7
8								8

© 2020 Cengage®. May not be scanned, copied or duplicated, or posted to a publicly accessible website, in whole or in part.

Name ______________________ Date ______________ Class ______________

22-1 WORK TOGETHER (concluded)

3.

CASH PAYMENTS JOURNAL

PAGE 10

					1	2	3	4	5	
	DATE	ACCOUNT TITLE	CK. NO.	POST. REF.	GENERAL DEBIT	GENERAL CREDIT	ACCOUNTS PAYABLE DEBIT	PURCHASES DISCOUNT CREDIT	CASH CREDIT	
1										1
2										2
3										3
4										4
5										5
6										6
7										7
8										8
9										9
10										10
11										11
12										12
13										13
14										14
15										15
16										16
17										17
18										18
19										19
20										20
21										21
22										22
23										23

© 2020 Cengage®. May not be scanned, copied or duplicated, or posted to a publicly accessible website, in whole or in part.

22-1 ON YOUR OWN (LO1, 2), p. 652

Calculating partnership earnings and journalizing partnership withdrawals

1. a. Percentage of total equity

	Partner's Equity	÷	Total Equity	=	Percentage of Total Equity
Greg Judson					
Pauline Malone					
Total equity					

	Total Net Income	×	Percentage of Total Equity	=	Share of Net Income
Greg Judson					
Pauline Malone					
Total net income					

1. b. Interest on equity plus fixed percentage

	Partner's Equity	×	Interest Rate	=	Interest on Equity
Greg Judson					
Pauline Malone					
Total interest					

Net Income	–	Total Interest	=	Remaining Net Income

	Remaining Net Income	×	Fixed Percentage	=	Partner's Share
Greg Judson					
Pauline Malone					
Total remaining net income					

	Interest on Equity	+	Remaining Net Income	=	Partner's Share
Greg Judson					
Pauline Malone					
Total net income					

© 2020 Cengage®. May not be scanned, copied or duplicated, or posted to a publicly accessible website, in whole or in part.

Name ______________________ Date ____________ Class ____________

22-1 ON YOUR OWN (continued)

2.

	Partner's Equity	×	Interest Rate	=	Interest on Equity
Greg Judson					
Pauline Malone					
Total interest					

Net Income	–	Total Interest	–	Total Salaries	=	Distribution Deficit

	Distribution Deficit	×	Fixed Percentage	=	Partner's Share
Greg Judson					
Pauline Malone					
Total distribution deficit					

	Interest on Equity	+	Salary	+	Distribution Deficit	=	Partner's Total Share
Greg Judson							
Pauline Malone							
Total net income							

3.

GENERAL JOURNAL PAGE 9

	DATE		ACCOUNT TITLE	DOC. NO.	POST. REF.	DEBIT	CREDIT	
1								1
2								2
3								3
4								4
5								5
6								6
7								7
8								8

© 2020 Cengage®. May not be scanned, copied or duplicated, or posted to a publicly accessible website, in whole or in part.

22-1 ON YOUR OWN (concluded)

3.

CASH PAYMENTS JOURNAL

PAGE 10

					1	2	3	4	5	
	DATE	ACCOUNT TITLE	CK. NO.	POST. REF.	GENERAL DEBIT	GENERAL CREDIT	ACCOUNTS PAYABLE DEBIT	PURCHASES DISCOUNT CREDIT	CASH CREDIT	
1										1
2										2
3										3
4										4
5										5
6										6
7										7
8										8
9										9
10										10
11										11
12										12
13										13
14										14
15										15
16										16
17										17
18										18
19										19
20										20
21										21
22										22
23										23

© 2020 Cengage®. May not be scanned, copied or duplicated, or posted to a publicly accessible website, in whole or in part.

Name ______________________ Date ____________ Class ____________

22-2 WORK TOGETHER (LO3), p. 657

End-of-period work for a partnership

1.

© 2020 Cengage®. May not be scanned, copied or duplicated, or posted to a publicly accessible website, in whole or in part.

22-2 WORK TOGETHER (concluded)

J&M Body Shop

2.

GENERAL JOURNAL PAGE 16

	DATE		ACCOUNT TITLE	DOC. NO.	POST. REF.	DEBIT	CREDIT	
1								1
2								2
3								3
4								4
5								5
6								6
7								7
8								8
9								9
10								10
11								11
12								12

© 2020 Cengage®. May not be scanned, copied or duplicated, or posted to a publicly accessible website, in whole or in part.

Name ______________________ Date ____________ Class ____________

22-2 ON YOUR OWN (LO3), p. 657

End-of-period work for a partnership

1.

© 2020 Cengage®. May not be scanned, copied or duplicated, or posted to a publicly accessible website, in whole or in part.

Kim's Gift Shop

2.

GENERAL JOURNAL PAGE 20

DATE		ACCOUNT TITLE	DOC. NO.	POST. REF.	DEBIT	CREDIT

© 2020 Cengage®. May not be scanned, copied or duplicated, or posted to a publicly accessible website, in whole or in part.

Name ____________ Date ____________ Class ____________

22-3 WORK TOGETHER (LO4), p. 663

Liquidation of a partnership

Cash	$12,500.00
Supplies	850.00
Equipment	12,500.00
Accumulated Depreciation—Equipment	6,900.00
Truck	28,600.00
Accumulated Depreciation—Truck	16,400.00
Accounts Payable	2,250.00
Mandi Stokes, Capital	14,600.00
Dustin Mann, Capital	14,300.00

CASH RECEIPTS JOURNAL PAGE 6

	DATE	ACCOUNT TITLE	DOC. NO.	POST. REF.	1 GENERAL DEBIT	2 GENERAL CREDIT	3 ACCOUNTS RECEIVABLE CREDIT	4 SALES CREDIT	5 SALES TAX PAYABLE CREDIT	6 SALES DISCOUNT DEBIT	7 CASH DEBIT	
1												1
2												2
3												3
4												4
5												5
6												6
7												7
8												8
9												9
10												10
11												11
12												12

© 2020 Cengage®. May not be scanned, copied or duplicated, or posted to a publicly accessible website, in whole or in part.

22-3 WORK TOGETHER (concluded)

GENERAL JOURNAL — PAGE 5

	DATE	ACCOUNT TITLE	DOC. NO.	POST. REF.	DEBIT	CREDIT	
1							1
2							2
3							3
4							4
5							5
6							6
7							7
8							8

CASH PAYMENTS JOURNAL — PAGE 5

					1	2	3	4	5	
	DATE	ACCOUNT TITLE	CK. NO.	POST. REF.	GENERAL DEBIT	GENERAL CREDIT	ACCOUNTS PAYABLE DEBIT	PURCHASES DISCOUNT CREDIT	CASH CREDIT	
1										1
2										2
3										3
4										4
5										5
6										6
7										7
8										8
9										9
10										10
11										11

© 2020 Cengage®. May not be scanned, copied or duplicated, or posted to a publicly accessible website, in whole or in part.

Name ____________________ Date ____________ Class ____________

22-3 ON YOUR OWN (LO4), p. 663

Cash	$ 7,780.00
Supplies	850.00
Equipment	16,500.00
Accumulated Depreciation—Equipment	8,625.00
Truck	28,750.00
Accumulated Depreciation—Truck	20,350.00
Accounts Payable	875.00
Petre Oakley, Capital	18,250.00
Jamal Beck, Capital	5,780.00

CASH RECEIPTS JOURNAL

PAGE 8

					1	2	3	4	5	6	7	
	DATE	ACCOUNT TITLE	DOC. NO.	POST. REF.	GENERAL DEBIT	GENERAL CREDIT	ACCOUNTS RECEIVABLE CREDIT	SALES CREDIT	SALES TAX PAYABLE CREDIT	SALES DISCOUNT DEBIT	CASH DEBIT	
1												1
2												2
3												3
4												4
5												5
6												6
7												7
8												8
9												9
10												10
11												11
12												12

© 2020 Cengage®. May not be scanned, copied or duplicated, or posted to a publicly accessible website, in whole or in part.

22-3 ON YOUR OWN (concluded)

GENERAL JOURNAL

PAGE 6

	DATE		ACCOUNT TITLE	DOC. NO.	POST. REF.	DEBIT	CREDIT	
1								1
2								2
3								3
4								4
5								5
6								6
7								7
8								8

CASH PAYMENTS JOURNAL

PAGE 10

					1	2	3	4	5	
	DATE		ACCOUNT TITLE	CK. NO.	POST. REF.	GENERAL		ACCOUNTS PAYABLE DEBIT	PURCHASES DISCOUNT CREDIT	CASH CREDIT	
					DEEIT	CREDIT				
1										1
2										2
3										3
4										4
5										5
6										6
7										7
8										8
9										9
10										10
11										11

© 2020 Cengage®. May not be scanned, copied or duplicated, or posted to a publicly accessible website, in whole or in part.

Name ______________________ Date ____________ Class ____________

22-1 APPLICATION PROBLEM (LO1, 2), p. 665

Calculating partnership earnings and journalizing partnership withdrawals

1. a. Fixed percentages:

1. b. Percentage of total equity

1. c. Interest on equity plus fixed percentage

© 2020 Cengage®. May not be scanned, copied or duplicated, or posted to a publicly accessible website, in whole or in part.

1. d. Salary and fixed percentage

© 2020 Cengage®. May not be scanned, copied or duplicated, or posted to a publicly accessible website, in whole or in part.

22-1 APPLICATION PROBLEM (continued)

1. e. Interest on equity, salary, and fixed percentage

© 2020 Cengage®. May not be scanned, copied or duplicated, or posted to a publicly accessible website, in whole or in part.

22-1 APPLICATION PROBLEM (continued)

1. f. Salary and fixed percentage

2.

GENERAL JOURNAL PAGE 9

	DATE		ACCOUNT TITLE	DOC. NO.	POST. REF.	DEBIT	CREDIT	
1								1
2								2
3								3
4								4
5								5
6								6
7								7
8								8

© 2020 Cengage®. May not be scanned, copied or duplicated, or posted to a publicly accessible website, in whole or in part.

Name ______________________ Date ____________ Class ____________

22-1 APPLICATION PROBLEM (concluded)

CASH PAYMENTS JOURNAL

PAGE 10

	DATE	ACCOUNT TITLE	CK. NO.	POST. REF.	1 GENERAL DEBIT	2 GENERAL CREDIT	3 ACCOUNTS PAYABLE DEBIT	4 PURCHASES DISCOUNT CREDIT	5 CASH CREDIT	
1										1
2										2
3										3
4										4
5										5
6										6
7										7
8										8
9										9
10										10
11										11
12										12
13										13
14										14
15										15
16										16
17										17
18										18
19										19
20										20
21										21
22										22
23										23

© 2020 Cengage®. May not be scanned, copied or duplicated, or posted to a publicly accessible website, in whole or in part.

22-2 APPLICATION PROBLEM (LO3), p. 665

End-of-period work for a partnership

1.

© 2020 Cengage®. May not be scanned, copied or duplicated, or posted to a publicly accessible website, in whole or in part.

Name ____________________ Date __________ Class __________

22-2 APPLICATION PROBLEM (concluded)

2.

Sherra's Home Health

Owners' Equity Statement

For the Year Ended December 31, 20--

3.

GENERAL JOURNAL PAGE 22

DATE		ACCOUNT TITLE	DOC. NO.	POST. REF.	DEBIT	CREDIT

© 2020 Cengage®. May not be scanned, copied or duplicated, or posted to a publicly accessible website, in whole or in part.

22-3 APPLICATION PROBLEM (LO4), p. 666

CASH RECEIPTS JOURNAL

PAGE 13

					1	2	3	4	5	6	7	
					GENERAL							
	DATE	ACCOUNT TITLE	DOC. NO.	POST. REF.	DEBIT	CREDIT	ACCOUNTS RECEIVABLE CREDIT	SALES CREDIT	SALES TAX PAYABLE CREDIT	SALES DISCOUNT DEBIT	CASH DEBIT	
1												1
2												2
3												3
4												4
5												5
6												6
7												7
8												8
9												9
10												10
11												11

GENERAL JOURNAL

PAGE 8

	DATE	ACCOUNT TITLE	DOC. NO.	POST. REF.	DEBIT	CREDIT	
1							1
2							2
3							3
4							4
5							5
6							6
7							7
8							8

© 2020 Cengage®. May not be scanned, copied or duplicated, or posted to a publicly accessible website, in whole or in part.

Name ______________________ Date ____________ Class ____________

22-3 APPLICATION PROBLEM (concluded)

CASH PAYMENTS JOURNAL

PAGE 13

	DATE	ACCOUNT TITLE	CK. NO.	POST. REF.	1 GENERAL DEBIT	2 GENERAL CREDIT	3 ACCOUNTS PAYABLE DEBIT	4 PURCHASES DISCOUNT CREDIT	5 CASH CREDIT	
1										1
2										2
3										3
4										4
5										5
6										6
7										7
8										8
9										9
10										10
11										11
12										12
13										13
14										14
15										15
16										16
17										17
18										18
19										19

© 2020 Cengage®. May not be scanned, copied or duplicated, or posted to a publicly accessible website, in whole or in part.

22-M MASTERY PROBLEM (LO1, 3), p. 667

Completing end-of-period work for a partnership

1.

© 2020 Cengage®. May not be scanned, copied or duplicated, or posted to a publicly accessible website, in whole or in part.

Name ____________________ Date ____________ Class ____________

22-M MASTERY PROBLEM (concluded)

2.

Dean's Gym

Owners' Equity Statement

For the Year Ended December 31, 20--

3.

GENERAL JOURNAL PAGE 18

DATE		ACCOUNT TITLE	DOC. NO.	POST. REF.	DEBIT	CREDIT

© 2020 Cengage®. May not be scanned, copied or duplicated, or posted to a publicly accessible website, in whole or in part.

22-C CHALLENGE PROBLEM (LO1, 3), p. 667

Completing end-of-period work for a partnership

C&N Plumbing

Adjusted Trial Balance

December 31, 20--

ACCOUNT TITLE	DEBIT	CREDIT
Cash	5 1 5 3 50	
Accounts Receivable	18 6 7 1 31	
Allowance for Uncollectible Accounts		3 2 5 0 00
Supplies	6 4 8 00	
Equipment	32 1 5 4 90	
Accumulated Depreciation—Equipment		20 5 0 0 00
Car	24 5 3 2 00	
Accumulated Depreciation—Car		16 2 0 0 00
Accounts Payable		1 9 8 4 20
Line of Credit		5 0 0 0 00
Johan Copeland, Capital		32 4 5 0 60
Johan Copeland, Drawing	22 0 0 0 00	
Lou Newell, Capital		28 4 5 7 74
Lou Newell, Drawing	18 2 0 0 00	
Sales		64 8 1 4 62
Advertising Expense	16 4 8 1 15	
Depreciation Expense—Car	4 2 0 0 00	
Depreciation Expense—Equipment	5 4 0 0 00	
Insurance Expense	6 4 5 0 00	
Miscellaneous Expense	9 1 5 4 89	
Supplies Expense	3 5 1 5 21	
Uncollectible Accounts Expense	9 4 8 15	
Utilities Expense	5 1 4 8 05	
	172 6 5 7 16	172 6 5 7 16

© 2020 Cengage®. May not be scanned, copied or duplicated, or posted to a publicly accessible website, in whole or in part.

Name ____________ Date ____________ Class ____________

22-C CHALLENGE PROBLEM (continued)

1.

C&N Plumbing

Income Statement

For the Year Ended December 31, 20--

			% OF SALES*

© 2020 Cengage®. May not be scanned, copied or duplicated, or posted to a publicly accessible website, in whole or in part.

2.

© 2020 Cengage®. May not be scanned, copied or duplicated, or posted to a publicly accessible website, in whole or in part.

Name ______________ Date ______________ Class ______________

22-C CHALLENGE PROBLEM (continued)

3.

C&N Plumbing

Owners' Equity Statement

For the Year Ended December 31, 20--

© 2020 Cengage®. May not be scanned, copied or duplicated, or posted to a publicly accessible website, in whole or in part.

22-C CHALLENGE PROBLEM (concluded)

4.

C&N Plumbing

Balance Sheet

December 31, 20--

© 2020 Cengage®. May not be scanned, copied or duplicated, or posted to a publicly accessible website, in whole or in part.

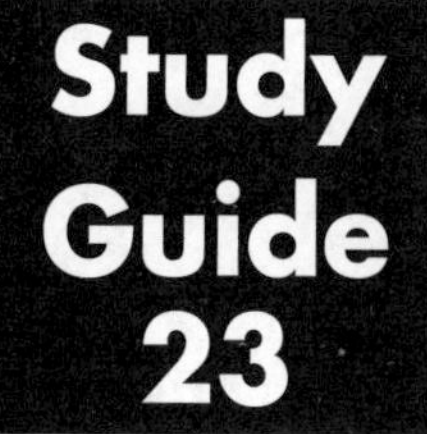

Name	Perfect Score	Your Score
Identifying Accounting Terms	11 Pts.	
Analyzing Accounting Practices of a Not-for-Profit Organization	15 Pts.	
Analyzing Transactions for a Governmental Organization	28 Pts.	
Total	54 Pts.	

Part One—Identifying Accounting Terms

Directions: Select the one term in Column I that best fits each definition in Column II. Print the letter identifying your choice in the Answers column.

Column I	Column II	Answers
A. appropriations	**1.** An organization providing goods or services with neither a conscious motive nor an expectation of earning a profit. (p. 672)	**1.** ______
B. certificate of deposit	**2.** A governmental accounting entity with a set of accounts in which assets always equal liabilities plus equities. (p. 675)	**2.** ______
C. expenditures	**3.** Cash disbursements and liabilities incurred for the cost of goods delivered or services rendered. (p. 676)	**3.** ______
D. encumbrance	**4.** A statement that reports the sources of revenues and the expenditure of funds of a government organization. (p. 676)	**4.** ______
E. fund	**5.** The amount of assets less liabilities of a governmental organization. (p. 676)	**5.** ______
F. fund equity	**6.** A plan of current expenditures and the proposed means of financing those expenditures. (p. 678)	**6.** ______
G. general fixed assets	**7.** Authorizations to make expenditures for specific purposes. (p. 680)	**7.** ______
H. not-for-profit organization	**8.** Authorized action taken by a governmental organization to collect taxes by legal authority. (p. 683)	**8.** ______
I. operating budget	**9.** A commitment to pay for goods or services that have been ordered but not yet provided. (p. 687)	**9.** ______
J. statement of revenues, expenditures, and changes in fund balance	**10.** Governmental properties that benefit future periods. (p. 690)	**10.** ______
K. tax levy	**11.** A document issued by a bank as evidence of money invested with the bank. (p. 691)	**11.** ______

© 2020 Cengage®. May not be scanned, copied or duplicated, or posted to a publicly accessible website, in whole or in part.

Part Two—Analyzing Accounting Practices of a Not-for-Profit Organization

Directions: Place a *T* for True or *F* for False in the Answers column to show whether each of the following statements is true or false.

	Answers
1. Business organizations differ in their kinds of ownership, but they have a common objective—to earn a profit. (p. 672)	**1.** ______
2. Since a governmental organization does not intend to earn a profit from its operation, success is easy to measure. (p. 674)	**2.** ______
3. Both business and governmental organizations apply the accounting equation, assets equal liabilities plus equity. (p. 674)	**3.** ______
4. The fund balance for a governmental organization is reported as assets plus liabilities. (p. 675)	**4.** ______
5. Revenues for a governmental organization are recorded only when cash is received. (p. 675)	**5.** ______
6. Preparing financial statements for a governmental organization at the end of a fiscal period is an application of the Accounting Period Cycle concept. (p. 676)	**6.** ______
7. Expenditures for a governmental organization are recorded in the accounting period in which money is spent or liabilities incurred. (p. 676)	**7.** ______
8. Approval of an annual governmental operating budget by the proper authorities provides legal authorization for expenditures to be made in accordance with the approved budget. (p. 680)	**8.** ______
9. In governmental accounting, appropriations should always equal estimated revenues. (p. 681)	**9.** ______
10. In governmental accounting, appropriations are the same as expenditures. (p. 681)	**10.** ______
11. Levied property taxes are considered measurable and available because they become a legal obligation of property owners. (p. 687)	**11.** ______
12. Some revenues, such as fines, inspection charges, parking meter receipts, and penalties, are normally not known and, thus, are not measurable until cash is received. (p. 684)	**12.** ______
13. An encumbrance is recorded when an invoice for goods and services is received from the vendor. (p. 687)	**13.** ______
14. Expenditures plus encumbrances for a specific account equal the total commitment that has been made against the appropriated amount for that account. (p. 688)	**14.** ______
15. When a city repays a note payable, the amount of the interest paid is recorded as Interest Expense. (p. 690)	**15.** ______

© 2020 Cengage®. May not be scanned, copied or duplicated, or posted to a publicly accessible website, in whole or in part.

Name ______________________ Date ____________ Class ____________

Part Three—Analyzing Transactions for a Governmental Organization

Directions: For each transaction below, print in the proper Answers column the identifying letters of the accounts to be debited and credited.

Account Titles

A. Allowance for Uncollectible Taxes—Current
B. Allowance for Uncollectible Taxes—Delinquent
C. Appropriations
D. Budgetary Fund Balance
E. Cash
F. Encumbrance—Supplies, General Government
G. Estimated Revenues
H. Expenditure—Capital Outlays, General Government
I. Expenditure—Other Charges, General Government
J. Expenditure—Personnel, General Government
K. Expenditure—Supplies, General Government
L. Interest Revenue
M. Investments—Short Term
N. Notes Payable
O. Other Revenue
P. Property Tax Revenue
Q. Reserve for Encumbrances—Current Year
R. Taxes Receivable—Current
S. Taxes Receivable—Delinquent

Transactions	Answers Debit	Answers Credit
1-2. Recorded current year's approved operating budget. (p. 681)	1. ______	2. ______
3-4. Recorded current year's property tax levy. (p. 683)	3. ______	4. ______
5-6. Received cash for current taxes receivable. (p. 684)	5. ______	6. ______
7-8. Received cash for traffic fines. (p. 684)	7. ______	8. ______
9-10. Recorded reclassification of current taxes receivable to delinquent status and accompanying allowance accounts. (p. 685)	9. ______	10. ______
11-12. Received cash for delinquent taxes receivable. (p. 685)	11. ______	12. ______
13-14. Paid cash for gas utility service. (p. 687)	13. ______	14. ______
15-16. Encumbered estimated amount for supplies. (p. 688)	15. ______	16. ______
17-18. Paid cash for supplies previously encumbered. (p. 689)	17. ______	18. ______
19-20. Paid cash for property benefiting future periods. (pp. 689–690)	19. ______	20. ______
21-22. Issued a note payable. (p. 690)	21. ______	22. ______
23-24. Paid note payable plus interest. (p. 690)	23. ______	24. ______
25-26. Paid cash for a certificate of deposit. (p. 691)	25. ______	26. ______
27-28. Received cash plus interest for certificate of deposit due today. (p. 692)	27. ______	28. ______

© 2020 Cengage®. May not be scanned, copied or duplicated, or posted to a publicly accessible website, in whole or in part.

Name ______________________ Date ____________ Class ____________

23-1 WORK TOGETHER (LO4), p. 682

Journalizing governmental operating budgets

JOURNAL PAGE 1

	DATE		ACCOUNT TITLE	DOC. NO.	POST. REF.	GENERAL DEBIT (1)	GENERAL CREDIT (2)	CASH DEBIT (3)	CASH CREDIT (4)	
1										1
2										2
3										3
4										4
5										5
6										6
7										7
8										8
9										9
10										10
11										11
12										12
13										13
14										14
15										15
16										16
17										17
18										18
19										19
20										20
21										21
22										22
23										23

© 2020 Cengage®. May not be scanned, copied or duplicated, or posted to a publicly accessible website, in whole or in part.

23-1 ON YOUR OWN (LO4), p. 682

Journalizing governmental operating budgets

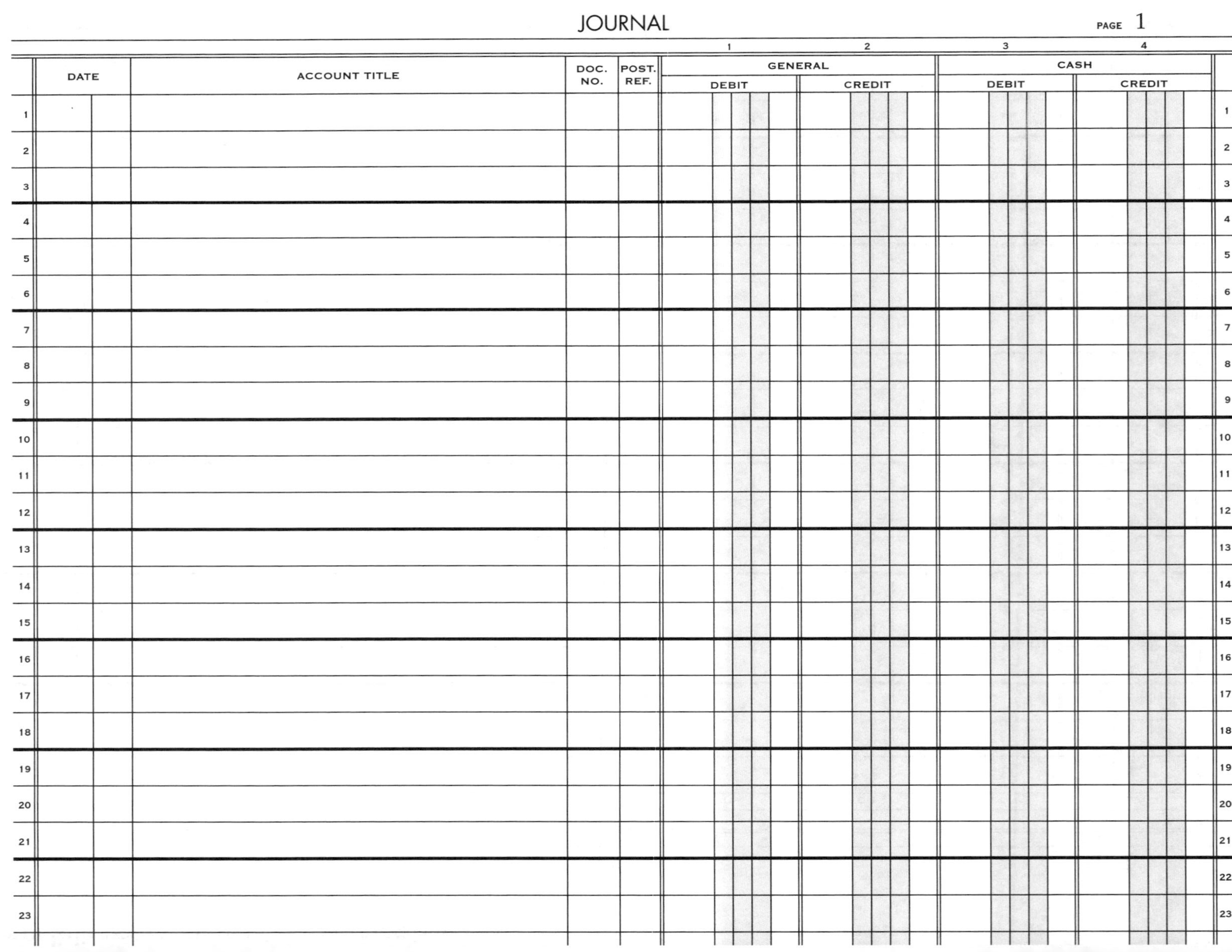

JOURNAL PAGE 1

	DATE		ACCOUNT TITLE	DOC. NO.	POST. REF.	GENERAL DEBIT (1)	GENERAL CREDIT (2)	CASH DEBIT (3)	CASH CREDIT (4)	
1										1
2										2
3										3
4										4
5										5
6										6
7										7
8										8
9										9
10										10
11										11
12										12
13										13
14										14
15										15
16										16
17										17
18										18
19										19
20										20
21										21
22										22
23										23

© 2020 Cengage®. May not be scanned, copied or duplicated, or posted to a publicly accessible website, in whole or in part.

Name ____________________ Date ____________ Class ____________

23-2 WORK TOGETHER (LO5), p. 686

Journalizing governmental revenue transactions

JOURNAL

PAGE 1

	DATE	ACCOUNT TITLE	DOC. NO.	POST. REF.	GENERAL DEBIT (1)	GENERAL CREDIT (2)	CASH DEBIT (3)	CASH CREDIT (4)	
1									1
2									2
3									3
4									4
5									5
6									6
7									7
8									8
9									9
10									10
11									11
12									12
13									13
14									14
15									15
16									16
17									17
18									18
19									19
20									20
21									21
22									22
23									23

© 2020 Cengage®. May not be scanned, copied or duplicated, or posted to a publicly accessible website, in whole or in part.

23-2 ON YOUR OWN (LO5), p. 686

Journalizing governmental revenue transactions

JOURNAL

PAGE 1

	DATE	ACCOUNT TITLE	DOC. NO.	POST. REF.	GENERAL DEBIT (1)	GENERAL CREDIT (2)	CASH DEBIT (3)	CASH CREDIT (4)	
1									1
2									2
3									3
4									4
5									5
6									6
7									7
8									8
9									9
10									10
11									11
12									12
13									13
14									14
15									15
16									16
17									17
18									18
19									19
20									20
21									21
22									22
23									23

© 2020 Cengage®. May not be scanned, copied or duplicated, or posted to a publicly accessible website, in whole or in part.

Name ______________________ Date ____________ Class ____________

23-3 WORK TOGETHER (LO6, 7), p. 693

Journalizing governmental encumbrances, expenditures, and other transactions

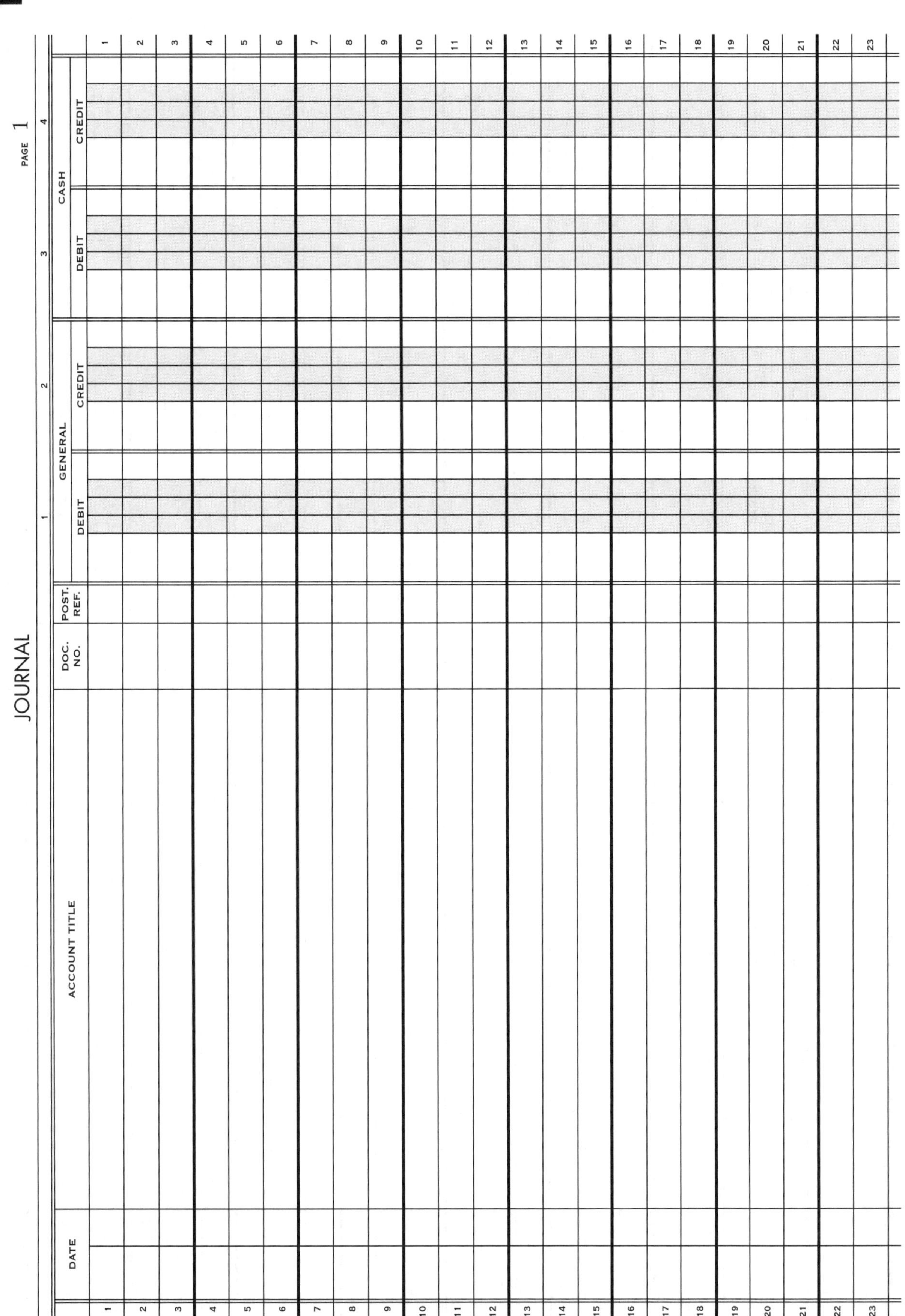

JOURNAL PAGE 1

	DATE	ACCOUNT TITLE	DOC. NO.	POST. REF.	GENERAL DEBIT (1)	GENERAL CREDIT (2)	CASH DEBIT (3)	CASH CREDIT (4)	
1									1
2									2
3									3
4									4
5									5
6									6
7									7
8									8
9									9
10									10
11									11
12									12
13									13
14									14
15									15
16									16
17									17
18									18
19									19
20									20
21									21
22									22
23									23

© 2020 Cengage®. May not be scanned, copied or duplicated, or posted to a publicly accessible website, in whole or in part.

23-3 ON YOUR OWN (LO6, 7), p. 693

Journalizing governmental encumbrances, expenditures, and other transactions

JOURNAL PAGE 1

				1	2	3	4	
				GENERAL		CASH		
DATE	ACCOUNT TITLE	DOC. NO.	POST. REF.	DEBIT	CREDIT	DEBIT	CREDIT	
1								1
2								2
3								3
4								4
5								5
6								6
7								7
8								8
9								9
10								10
11								11
12								12
13								13
14								14
15								15
16								16
17								17
18								18
19								19
20								20
21								21
22								22
23								23

© 2020 Cengage®. May not be scanned, copied or duplicated, or posted to a publicly accessible website, in whole or in part.

Name ______________________ Date ______________ Class ______________

23-1 APPLICATION PROBLEM (LO4), p. 695

Journalizing governmental operating budgets

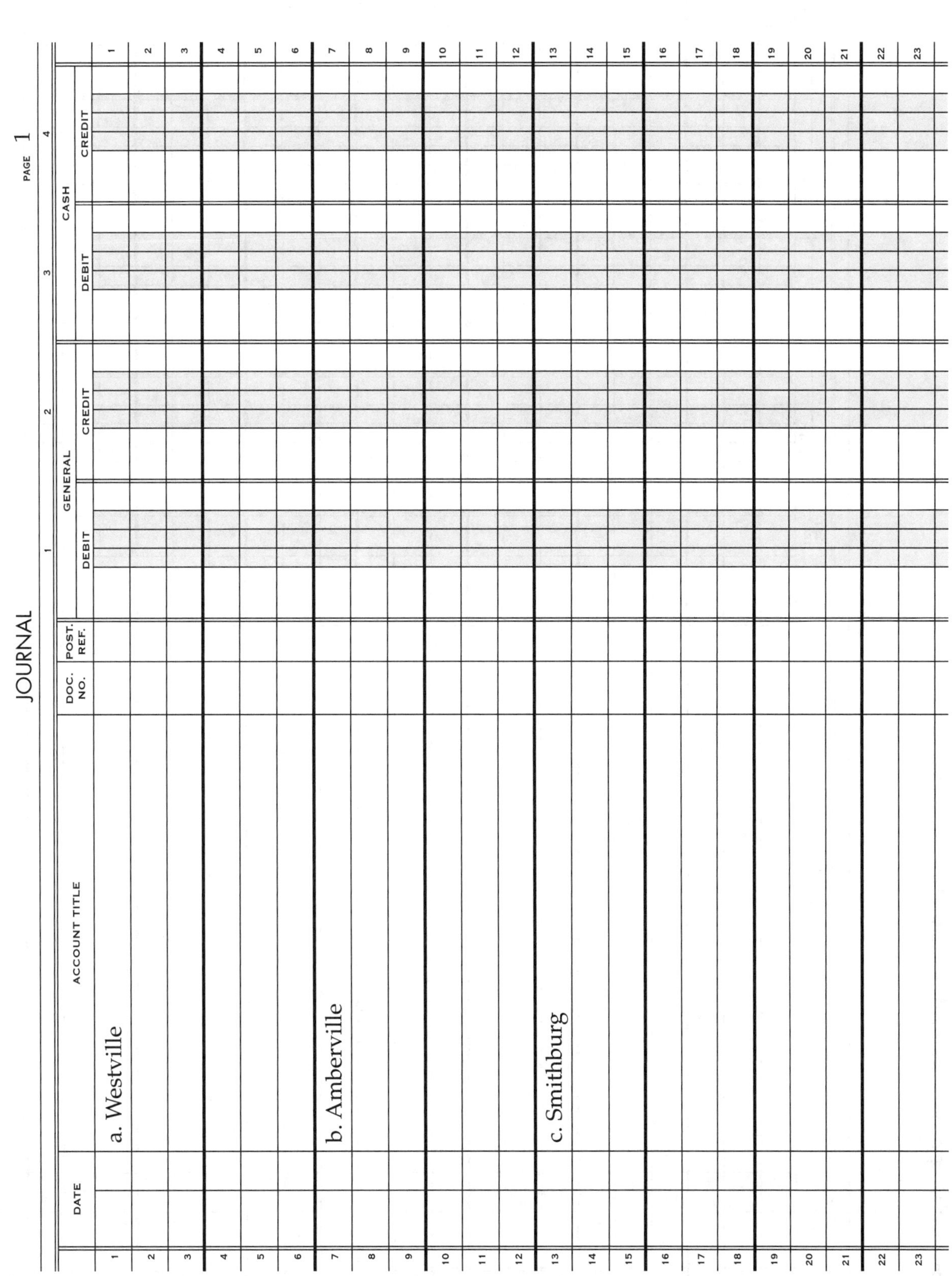

JOURNAL PAGE 1

	DATE	ACCOUNT TITLE	DOC. NO.	POST. REF.	GENERAL DEBIT (1)	GENERAL CREDIT (2)	CASH DEBIT (3)	CASH CREDIT (4)	
1		a. Westville							1
2									2
3									3
4									4
5									5
6									6
7		b. Amberville							7
8									8
9									9
10									10
11									11
12									12
13		c. Smithburg							13
14									14
15									15
16									16
17									17
18									18
19									19
20									20
21									21
22									22
23									23

© 2020 Cengage®. May not be scanned, copied or duplicated, or posted to a publicly accessible website, in whole or in part.

23-2 APPLICATION PROBLEM (LO5), p. 695

Journalizing governmental revenue transactions

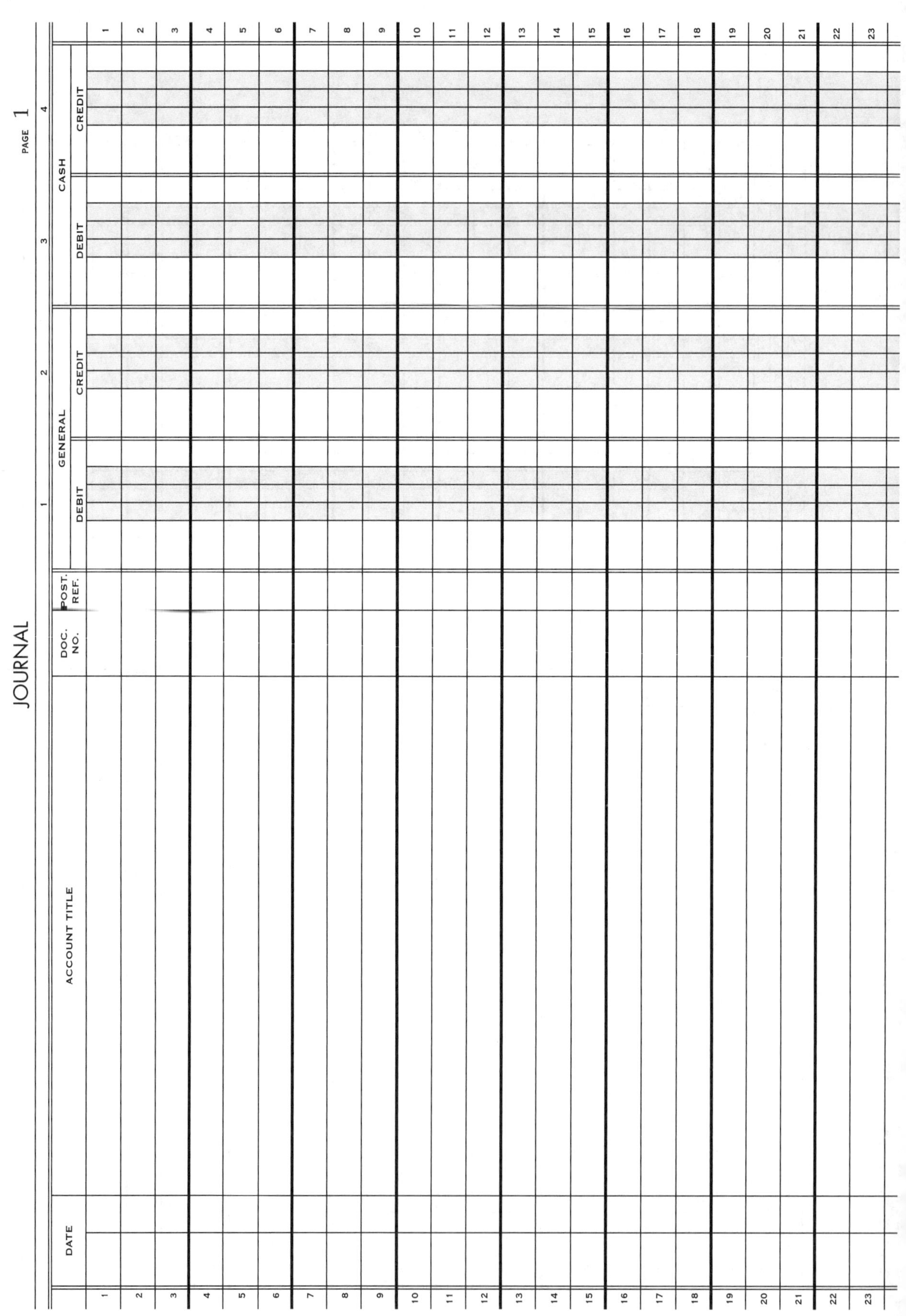

© 2020 Cengage®. May not be scanned, copied or duplicated, or posted to a publicly accessible website, in whole or in part.

Name ____________________ Date ____________ Class ____________

23-3 APPLICATION PROBLEM (LO6, 7), p. 696

Journalizing governmental encumbrances, expenditures, and other transactions

JOURNAL

PAGE

				1	2	3	4
				GENERAL		CASH	
DATE	ACCOUNT TITLE	DOC. NO.	POST. REF.	DEBIT	CREDIT	DEBIT	CREDIT

© 2020 Cengage®. May not be scanned, copied or duplicated, or posted to a publicly accessible website, in whole or in part.

23-M MASTERY PROBLEM (LO4, 5, 6, 7), p. 696

Journalizing governmental transactions

JOURNAL

PAGE

	DATE	ACCOUNT TITLE	DOC. NO.	POST. REF.	GENERAL DEBIT (1)	GENERAL CREDIT (2)	CASH DEBIT (3)	CASH CREDIT (4)	
1									1
2									2
3									3
4									4
5									5
6									6
7									7
8									8
9									9
10									10
11									11
12									12
13									13
14									14
15									15
16									16
17									17
18									18
19									19
20									20
21									21
22									22
23									23
24									24

© 2020 Cengage®. May not be scanned, copied or duplicated, or posted to a publicly accessible website, in whole or in part.

Name ______________________ Date ____________ Class ____________

23-M MASTERY PROBLEM (concluded)

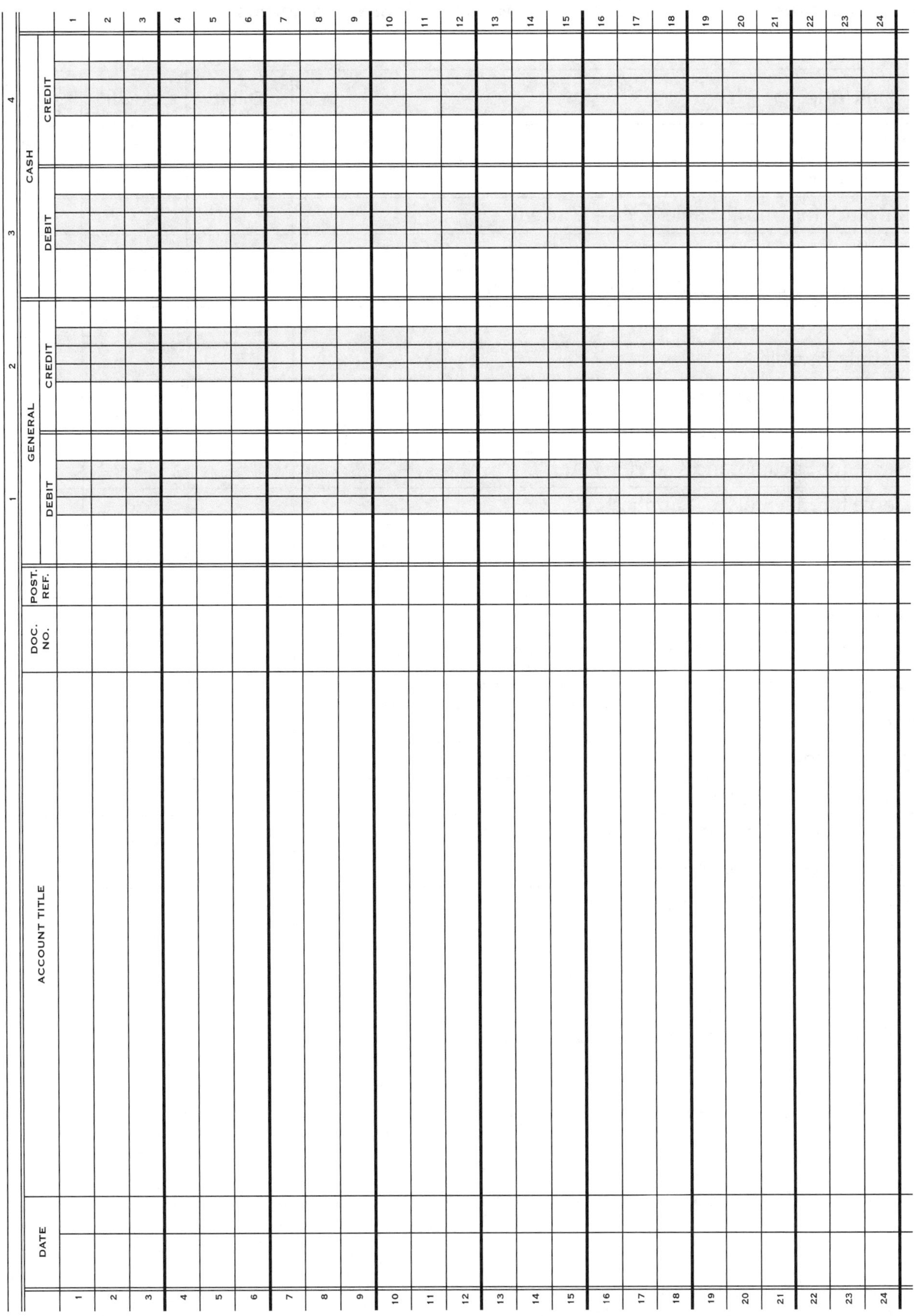

© 2020 Cengage®. May not be scanned, copied or duplicated, or posted to a publicly accessible website, in whole or in part.

23-C CHALLENGE PROBLEM (LO4, 5, 6), p. 697

Determining the increase, decrease, and normal balance of accounts

Account Title	Debit	Credit	Normal Balance
Cash	+	–	Dr.
Taxes Receivable—Current			
Allowance for Uncollectible Taxes—Current			
Taxes Receivable—Delinquent			
Allowance for Uncollectible Taxes—Delinquent			
Inventory of Supplies			
Accounts Payable			
Unreserved Fund Balance			
Reserve for Encumbrances—Current Year			
Reserve for Encumbrances—Prior Year			
Reserve for Inventory of Supplies			
Property Tax Revenue			
Other Revenue			
Expenditure—Personnel, General Government			
Expenditure—Supplies, General Government			
Expenditure—Other Charges, General Government			
Estimated Revenues			
Appropriations			
Budgetary Fund Balance			
Encumbrance—Personnel, General Government			
Encumbrance—Supplies, General Government			
Encumbrance—Other Charges, General Government			

© 2020 Cengage®. May not be scanned, copied or duplicated, or posted to a publicly accessible website, in whole or in part.

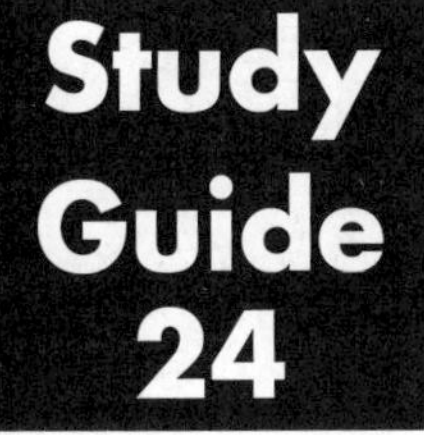

Name	Perfect Score	Your Score
Analyzing End-of-Period Work for a Governmental Organization	8 Pts.	
Classifying Items on a Governmental Organization's Financial Statements	32 Pts.	
Analyzing Adjusting and Closing Entries for a Not-or-Profit Organization	14 Pts.	
Total	54 Pts.	

Part One—Analyzing End-of-Period Work for a Governmental Organization

Directions: For each item below, select the choice that best completes the sentence. Print the letter identifying your choice in the Answers column.

Answers

1. Governmental funds do not record or report (p. 704) **1.** ______
- **a.** assets
- **b.** expenditures
- **c.** expenses
- **d.** liabilities

2. When supplies are bought (p. 704) **2.** ______
- **a.** an expenditure account is debited
- **b.** an expense account is debited
- **c.** an asset account is debited
- **d.** a fund balance account is debited

3. At the end of a fiscal period, an adjustment is made to record the amount of supplies on hand as (p. 704) **3.** ______
- **a.** a fund balance
- **b.** an expense
- **c.** an expenditure
- **d.** an asset

4. Governmental funds recognize revenues when the revenues (p. 705) **4.** ______
- **a.** are budgeted
- **b.** are collected
- **c.** are earned
- **d.** become measurable and available

5. When orders encumbered in the prior year are received, the amount paid is (p. 705) **5.** ______
- **a.** debited to Reserve for Encumbrances—Prior Year
- **b.** debited to Expenditures
- **c.** credited to Reserve for Encumbrances—Prior Year
- **d.** debited to Reserve for Encumbrances—Current Year

6. Which of the following accounts would not appear on a post-closing trial balance of a city government? (p. 711) **6.** ______
- **a.** Taxes Receivable--Delinquent
- **b.** Reserve for Inventory of Supplies
- **c.** Appropriations
- **d.** Accounts Payable

7. The financial statement on which state and local governments report each major fund as well as combined financial statements is the (p. 712) **7.** ______
- **a.** statement of activities
- **b.** consolidated financial statement
- **c.** comprehensive annual financial report
- **d.** GASB report

8. A fund that accounts for the financial transactions of a government organization that operates as a for-profit enterprise is a (p. 712) **8.** ______
- **a.** governmental fund
- **b.** proprietary fund
- **c.** fiduciary fund
- **d.** general fund

© 2020 Cengage®. May not be scanned, copied or duplicated, or posted to a publicly accessible website, in whole or in part.

Part Two—Classifying Items on a Governmental Organization's Financial Statements

Directions: Identify in which statement and in which section of that statement each item below will be reported. Write in the Answers column a letter from the Statement column and a number from the Statement Section column. The organization using these statements is a town.

Statement

A. Statement of Revenues, Expenditures, and Changes in Fund Balance—Budget and Actual

B. Balance Sheet

C. Neither A nor B

Statement Section

1. Assets
2. Expenditure
3. Fund Balance
4. Liabilities
5. Revenues
6. None of the above

Items	Answers: Statement	Answers: Statement Section
1-2. Accounts Payable (p. 709)	**1.** _______	**2.** _______
3-4. Allowance for Uncollectible Taxes—Delinquent (p. 709)	**3.** _______	**4.** _______
5-6. Appropriations (pp. 707–709)	**5.** _______	**6.** _______
7-8. Cash (p. 709)	**7.** _______	**8.** _______
9-10. Encumbrance—Supplies, Fire Protection (pp. 707–709)	**9.** _______	**10.** _______
11-12. Estimated Revenue (pp. 707–709)	**11.** _______	**12.** _______
13-14. Expenditures—Fire Protection (p. 707)	**13.** _______	**14.** _______
15-16. Interest Receivable (p. 709)	**15.** _______	**16.** _______
17-18. Interest Revenue (p. 707)	**17.** _______	**18.** _______
19-20. Inventory of Supplies (p. 709)	**19.** _______	**20.** _______
21-22. Notes Payable (p. 709)	**21.** _______	**22.** _______
23-24. Other Revenue (p. 707)	**23.** _______	**24.** _______
25-26. Property Tax Revenue (p. 707)	**25.** _______	**26.** _______
27-28. Reserve for Inventory of Supplies (p. 709)	**27.** _______	**28.** _______
29-30. Taxes Receivable—Delinquent (p. 709)	**29.** _______	**30.** _______
31-32. Total Fund Balance (p. 709)	**31.** _______	**32.** _______

© 2020 Cengage®. May not be scanned, copied or duplicated, or posted to a publicly accessible website, in whole or in part.

Name ______________________ Date ____________ Class ____________

Part Three—Analyzing Adjusting and Closing Entries for a Not-for-Profit Organization

Directions: For each entry below, print in the proper Answers columns the identifying letters of the accounts to be debited and credited.

Account Titles

A. Allowance for Uncollectible Interest

B. Appropriations

C. Budgetary Fund Balance

D. Encumbrance—Supplies, Recreation

E. Estimated Revenues

F. Expenditure—Personnel, Recreation

G. Interest Receivable

H. Interest Revenue

I. Inventory of Supplies

J. Property Tax Revenue

K. Reserve for Encumbrances—Current Year

L. Reserve for Encumbrances—Prior Year

M. Reserve for Inventory of Supplies

N. Unreserved Fund Balance

Transactions	Answers Debit	Answers Credit
1-2. Adjust for unused supplies on hand. (p. 704)	**1.** ______	**2.** ______
3-4. Adjust for interest revenue due but not collected. (p. 705)	**3.** ______	**4.** ______
5-6. Reclassify amount of encumbrances outstanding to prior year status. (p. 705)	**5.** ______	**6.** ______
7-8. Close revenue accounts. (p. 710)	**7.** ______	**8.** ______
9-10. Close expenditure accounts. (p. 710)	**9.** ______	**10.** ______
11-12. Close budgetary accounts. (p. 710)	**11.** ______	**12.** ______
13-14. Close outstanding encumbrance account. (p. 710)	**13.** ______	**14.** ______

© 2020 Cengage®. May not be scanned, copied or duplicated, or posted to a publicly accessible website, in whole or in part.

Name ____________________ Date ____________ Class ____________

24-1 WORK TOGETHER (LO1), p. 706

Preparing adjusting entries for a general fund

JOURNAL PAGE 22

	DATE	ACCOUNT TITLE	DOC. NO.	POST. REF.	1 GENERAL DEBIT	2 GENERAL CREDIT	3 CASH DEBIT	4 CASH CREDIT	
1									1
2									2
3									3
4									4
5									5
6									6
7									7
8									8
9									9
10									10
11									11
12									12
13									13
14									14
15									15
16									16
17									17
18									18
19									19
20									20
21									21
22									22
23									23

© 2020 Cengage®. May not be scanned, copied or duplicated, or posted to a publicly accessible website, in whole or in part.

24-1 ON YOUR OWN (LO1), p. 706

Preparing adjusting entries for a general fund

JOURNAL

PAGE 17

	DATE	ACCOUNT TITLE	DOC. NO.	POST. REF.	GENERAL DEBIT (1)	GENERAL CREDIT (2)	CASH DEBIT (3)	CASH CREDIT (4)	
1									1
2									2
3									3
4									4
5									5
6									6
7									7
8									8
9									9
10									10
11									11
12									12
13									13
14									14
15									15
16									16
17									17
18									18
19									19
20									20
21									21
22									22
23									23

© 2020 Cengage®. May not be scanned, copied or duplicated, or posted to a publicly accessible website, in whole or in part.

Name ______________ Date ______ Class ______

24-2 WORK TOGETHER (LO2, 3, 4), p. 714

Preparing financial statements for a governmental organization

City of River Springs
Annual Operating Budget—General Fund
For Year Ended December 31, 20--

ESTIMATED REVENUES		
Property Tax	$2,010,000.00	
Interest	16,400.00	
Other	8,200.00	
Total Estimated Revenues		$2,034,600.00
ESTIMATED EXPENDITURES AND BUDGETARY FUND BALANCE		
General Government		
Personnel	$ 325,320.00	
Supplies	28,720.00	
Other Charges	137,280.00	
Capital Outlays	28,680.00	
Total General Government		$ 520,000.00
Public Safety		
Personnel	$ 717,000.00	
Supplies	34,560.00	
Other Charges	173,240.00	
Capital Outlays	115,200.00	
Total Public Safety		1,040,000.00
Fire Protection		
Personnel	$ 138,600.00	
Supplies	16,080.00	
Other Charges	66,680.00	
Capital Outlays	68,640.00	
Total Fire Protection		290,000.00
Recreation		
Personnel	$ 75,960.00	
Supplies	6,200.00	
Other Charges	34,680.00	
Capital Outlays	23,160.00	
Total Recreation		140,000.00
Total Estimated Expenditures		$1,990,000.00
Budgetary Fund Balance		44,600.00
Total Estimated Expenditures and Budgetary Fund Balance		$2,034,600.00

© 2020 Cengage®. May not be scanned, copied or duplicated, or posted to a publicly accessible website, in whole or in part.

City of River Springs
Adjusted Trial Balance
December 31, 20--

ACCOUNT TITLE	DEBIT	CREDIT
Cash	74,620.00	
Taxes Receivable—Current		
Allowance for Uncollectible Taxes—Current		
Taxes Receivable—Delinquent	25,990.00	
Allowance for Uncollectible Taxes—Delinquent		20,090.00
Interest Receivable	3,840.00	
Allowance for Uncollectible Interest		1,540.00
Inventory of Supplies	3,300.00	
Accounts Payable		34,720.00
Notes Payable		
Unreserved Fund Balance		16,320.00
Reserve for Encumbrances—Current Year		
Reserve for Encumbrances—Prior Year		2,630.00
Reserve for Inventory of Supplies		3,300.00
Property Tax Revenue		2010,000.00
Interest Revenue		15,340.00
Other Revenue		7,370.00
Expenditure—Personnel, General Government	327,840.00	
Expenditure—Supplies, General Government	17,880.00	
Expenditure—Other Charges, General Government	142,060.00	
Expenditure—Capital Outlays, General Government	27,540.00	
Expenditure—Personnel, Public Safety	718,380.00	
Expenditure—Supplies, Public Safety	34,550.00	
Expenditure—Other Charges, Public Safety	180,960.00	
Expenditure—Capital Outlays, Public Safety	119,220.00	
Expenditure—Personnel, Fire Protection	147,960.00	
Expenditure—Supplies, Fire Protection	17,040.00	
Expenditure—Other Charges, Fire Protection	61,620.00	
Expenditure—Capital Outlays, Fire Protection	64,740.00	
Expenditure—Personnel, Recreation	75,120.00	
Expenditure—Supplies, Recreation	8,460.00	
Expenditure—Other Charges, Recreation	31,780.00	
Expenditure—Capital Outlays, Recreation	25,780.00	
Estimated Revenues	2034,600.00	
Appropriations		1990,000.00
Budgetary Fund Balance		44,600.00
Encumbrance—Supplies, General Government	2,630.00	
Totals	4145,910.00	4145,910.00

© 2020 Cengage®. May not be scanned, copied or duplicated, or posted to a publicly accessible website, in whole or in part.

Name ______________________ Date ____________ Class ____________

24-2 WORK TOGETHER (continued)

1.

	BUDGET	ACTUAL	VARIANCE— FAVORABLE (UNFAVORABLE)

© 2020 Cengage®. May not be scanned, copied or duplicated, or posted to a publicly accessible website, in whole or in part.

24-2 WORK TOGETHER (continued)

2.

© 2020 Cengage®. May not be scanned, copied or duplicated, or posted to a publicly accessible website, in whole or in part.

Name ______________________ Date ______________ Class ______________

24-2 WORK TOGETHER (continued)

JOURNAL

PAGE 21

DATE	ACCOUNT TITLE	DOC. NO.	POST. REF.	GENERAL DEBIT (1)	GENERAL CREDIT (2)	CASH DEBIT (3)	CASH CREDIT (4)

© 2020 Cengage®. May not be scanned, copied or duplicated, or posted to a publicly accessible website, in whole or in part.

24-2 WORK TOGETHER (concluded)

4.

© 2020 Cengage®. May not be scanned, copied or duplicated, or posted to a publicly accessible website, in whole or in part.

Name ______________________ Date ____________ Class ____________

24-2 ON YOUR OWN (LO2, 3, 4), p. 714

Preparing financial statements for a governmental organization

Town of Parson
Annual Operating Budget—General Fund
For Year Ended December 31, 20--

ESTIMATED REVENUES		
Property Tax	$1,050,000.00	
Interest	8,300.00	
Other	16,200.00	
Total Estimated Revenues		$1,074,500.00
ESTIMATED EXPENDITURES AND BUDGETARY FUND BALANCE		
General Government		
Personnel	$ 195,200.00	
Supplies	10,300.00	
Other Charges	82,400.00	
Capital Outlays	42,600.00	
Total General Government		$ 330,500.00
Public Safety		
Personnel	$ 330,200.00	
Supplies	20,700.00	
Other Charges	56,200.00	
Capital Outlays	48,000.00	
Total Public Safety		455,100.00
Fire Protection		
Personnel	$ 83,200.00	
Supplies	9,600.00	
Other Charges	40,000.00	
Capital Outlays	41,200.00	
Total Fire Protection		174,000.00
Recreation		
Personnel	$ 45,600.00	
Supplies	13,700.00	
Other Charges	20,800.00	
Capital Outlays	33,900.00	
Total Recreation		114,000.00
Total Estimated Expenditures		$1,073,600.00
Budgetary Fund Balance		900.00
Total Estimated Expenditures and Budgetary Fund Balance		$1,074,500.00

© 2020 Cengage®. May not be scanned, copied or duplicated, or posted to a publicly accessible website, in whole or in part.

Town of Parson

Adjusted Trial Balance

December 31, 20--

ACCOUNT TITLE	DEBIT	CREDIT
Cash	53,832.00	
Taxes Receivable—Current		
Allowance for Uncollectible Taxes—Current		
Taxes Receivable—Delinquent	16,890.00	
Allowance for Uncollectible Taxes—Delinquent		12,480.00
Interest Receivable	2,650.00	
Allowance for Uncollectible Interest		680.00
Inventory of Supplies	3,300.00	
Accounts Payable		20,182.00
Notes Payable		
Unreserved Fund Balance		24,680.00
Reserve for Encumbrances—Current Year		
Reserve for Encumbrances—Prior Year		13,250.00
Reserve for Inventory of Supplies		3,300.00
Property Tax Revenue		1,050,000.00
Interest Revenue		7,388.00
Other Revenue		16,784.00
Expenditure—Personnel, General Government	197,152.00	
Expenditure—Supplies, General Government	9,785.00	
Expenditure—Other Charges, General Government	80,752.00	
Expenditure—Capital Outlays, General Government	43,452.00	
Expenditure—Personnel, Public Safety	326,898.00	
Expenditure—Supplies, Public Safety	19,665.00	
Expenditure—Other Charges, Public Safety	57,886.00	
Expenditure—Capital Outlays, Public Safety	46,080.00	
Expenditure—Personnel, Fire Protection	79,040.00	
Expenditure—Supplies, Fire Protection	9,216.00	
Expenditure—Other Charges, Fire Protection	40,800.00	
Expenditure—Capital Outlays, Fire Protection	40,376.00	
Expenditure—Personnel, Recreation	47,880.00	
Expenditure—Supplies, Recreation	14,385.00	
Expenditure—Other Charges, Recreation	21,216.00	
Expenditure—Capital Outlays, Recreation	24,239.00	
Estimated Revenues	1,074,500.00	
Appropriations		1,073,600.00
Budgetary Fund Balance		900.00
Encumbrance—Capital Outlays, Recreation	13,250.00	
Totals	2,223,244.00	2,223,244.00

© 2020 Cengage®. May not be scanned, copied or duplicated, or posted to a publicly accessible website, in whole or in part.

Name ______________________ Date ____________ Class ____________

24-2 ON YOUR OWN (continued)

1.

	BUDGET	ACTUAL	VARIANCE— FAVORABLE (UNFAVORABLE)

© 2020 Cengage®. May not be scanned, copied or duplicated, or posted to a publicly accessible website, in whole or in part.

2.

© 2020 Cengage®. May not be scanned, copied or duplicated, or posted to a publicly accessible website, in whole or in part.

Name ______________________ Date ____________ Class ____________

24-2 ON YOUR OWN (continued)

3.

JOURNAL PAGE 24

	DATE		ACCOUNT TITLE	DOC. NO.	POST. REF.	GENERAL 1 DEBIT	GENERAL 2 CREDIT	CASH 3 DEBIT	CASH 4 CREDIT	
1										1
2										2
3										3
4										4
5										5
6										6
7										7
8										8
9										9
10										10
11										11
12										12
13										13
14										14
15										15
16										16
17										17
18										18
19										19
20										20
21										21
22										22
23										23
24										24
25										25
26										26
27										27

© 2020 Cengage®. May not be scanned, copied or duplicated, or posted to a publicly accessible website, in whole or in part.

24-2 ON YOUR OWN (concluded)

4.

© 2020 Cengage®. May not be scanned, copied or duplicated, or posted to a publicly accessible website, in whole or in part.

Name ______________________ Date ____________ Class ____________

24-1 APPLICATION PROBLEM (LO1), p. 716

Preparing adjusting entries for a governmental organizaton

JOURNAL

PAGE 26

	DATE	ACCOUNT TITLE	DOC. NO.	POST. REF.	GENERAL DEBIT (1)	GENERAL CREDIT (2)	CASH DEBIT (3)	CASH CREDIT (4)	
1									1
2									2
3									3
4									4
5									5
6									6
7									7
8									8
9									9
10									10
11									11
12									12
13									13
14									14
15									15
16									16
17									17
18									18
19									19
20									20
21									21
22									22
23									23

© 2020 Cengage®. May not be scanned, copied or duplicated, or posted to a publicly accessible website, in whole or in part.

24-2 APPLICATION PROBLEM (LO2, 3, 4), p. 716

Preparing financial statements for a governmental organization

City of Proffit Bluff
Annual Operating Budget—General Fund
For Year Ended December 31, 20--

ESTIMATED REVENUES		
Property Tax	$1,482,000.00	
Interest	12,600.00	
Other	22,500.00	
Total Estimated Revenues		$1,517,100.00
ESTIMATED EXPENDITURES AND BUDGETARY FUND BALANCE		
General Government		
Personnel	$ 273,300.00	
Supplies	14,400.00	
Other Charges	115,400.00	
Capital Outlays	59,600.00	
Total General Government		$ 462,700.00
Public Safety		
Personnel	$ 462,300.00	
Supplies	29,000.00	
Other Charges	78,700.00	
Capital Outlays	67,200.00	
Total Public Safety		637,200.00
Fire Protection		
Personnel	$ 116,500.00	
Supplies	13,400.00	
Other Charges	56,000.00	
Capital Outlays	57,700.00	
Total Fire Protection		243,600.00
Recreation		
Personnel	$ 63,800.00	
Supplies	19,200.00	
Other Charges	29,100.00	
Capital Outlays	47,500.00	
Total Recreation		159,600.00
Total Estimated Expenditures		$1,503,100.00
Budgetary Fund Balance		14,000.00
Total Estimated Expenditures and Budgetary Fund Balance		$1,517,100.00

© 2020 Cengage®. May not be scanned, copied or duplicated, or posted to a publicly accessible website, in whole or in part.

24-2 APPLICATION PROBLEM (continued)

City of Proffit Bluff
Adjusted Trial Balance
December 31, 20--

ACCOUNT TITLE	DEBIT	CREDIT
Cash	30,851.00	
Taxes Receivable—Current		
Allowance for Uncollectible Taxes—Current		
Taxes Receivable—Delinquent	25,680.00	
Allowance for Uncollectible Taxes—Delinquent		9,500.00
Interest Receivable	2,350.00	
Allowance for Uncollectible Interest		700.00
Inventory of Supplies	3,560.00	
Accounts Payable		24,180.00
Notes Payable		
Unreserved Fund Balance		30,580.00
Reserve for Encumbrances—Current Year		
Reserve for Encumbrances—Prior Year		4,050.00
Reserve for Inventory of Supplies		3,560.00
Property Tax Revenue		1,482,000.00
Interest Revenue		10,520.00
Other Revenue		24,352.00
Expenditure—Personnel, General Government	281,499.00	
Expenditure—Supplies, General Government	14,544.00	
Expenditure—Other Charges, General Government	109,630.00	
Expenditure—Capital Outlays, General Government	59,600.00	
Expenditure—Personnel, Public Safety	485,415.00	
Expenditure—Supplies, Public Safety	27,840.00	
Expenditure—Other Charges, Public Safety	82,635.00	
Expenditure—Capital Outlays, Public Safety	64,512.00	
Expenditure—Personnel, Fire Protection	110,675.00	
Expenditure—Supplies, Fire Protection	12,998.00	
Expenditure—Other Charges, Fire Protection	54,320.00	
Expenditure—Capital Outlays, Fire Protection	60,585.00	
Expenditure—Personnel, Recreation	60,610.00	
Expenditure—Supplies, Recreation	18,240.00	
Expenditure—Other Charges, Recreation	29,973.00	
Expenditure—Capital Outlays, Recreation	49,875.00	
Estimated Revenues	1,517,100.00	
Appropriations		1,503,100.00
Budgetary Fund Balance		14,000.00
Encumbrance—Other Charges, Public Safety	4,050.00	
Totals	3,106,542.00	3,106,542.00

© 2020 Cengage®. May not be scanned, copied or duplicated, or posted to a publicly accessible website, in whole or in part.

24-2 APPLICATION PROBLEM (continued)

1.

	BUDGET	ACTUAL	VARIANCE—FAVORABLE (UNFAVORABLE)

© 2020 Cengage®. May not be scanned, copied or duplicated, or posted to a publicly accessible website, in whole or in part.

Name ______________________ Date ____________ Class ____________

24-2 APPLICATION PROBLEM (continued)

2.

© 2020 Cengage®. May not be scanned, copied or duplicated, or posted to a publicly accessible website, in whole or in part.

24-2 APPLICATION PROBLEM (continued)

3.

JOURNAL PAGE 30

	DATE	ACCOUNT TITLE	DOC. NO.	POST. REF.	GENERAL DEBIT (1)	GENERAL CREDIT (2)	CASH DEBIT (3)	CASH CREDIT (4)	
1									1
2									2
3									3
4									4
5									5
6									6
7									7
8									8
9									9
10									10
11									11
12									12
13									13
14									14
15									15
16									16
17									17
18									18
19									19
20									20
21									21
22									22
23									23
24									24
25									25
26									26
27									27

© 2020 Cengage®. May not be scanned, copied or duplicated, or posted to a publicly accessible website, in whole or in part.

Name ______ Date ______ Class ______

24-2 APPLICATION PROBLEM (concluded)

4.

© 2020 Cengage®. May not be scanned, copied or duplicated, or posted to a publicly accessible website, in whole or in part.

24-M MASTERY PROBLEM (LO1, 2, 3, 4), p. 716

Completing the end-of-period work for a governmental organization

1.

JOURNAL

PAGE 30

	DATE	ACCOUNT TITLE	DOC. NO.	POST. REF.	GENERAL DEBIT (1)	GENERAL CREDIT (2)	CASH DEBIT (3)	CASH CREDIT (4)	
1									1
2									2
3									3
4									4
5									5
6									6
7									7
8									8
9									9
10									10
11									11
12									12
13									13
14									14
15									15
16									16
17									17
18									18
19									19
20									20
21									21
22									22

© 2020 Cengage®. May not be scanned, copied or duplicated, or posted to a publicly accessible website, in whole or in part.

Name ____________________ Date ____________ Class ____________

24-M MASTERY PROBLEM (continued)

City of Moserville Annual Operating Budget—General Fund For Year Ended December 31, 20--		
ESTIMATED REVENUES		
Property Tax	$1,725,000.00	
Interest	10,000.00	
Other	25,000.00	
Total Estimated Revenues		$1,760,000.00
ESTIMATED EXPENDITURES AND BUDGETARY FUND BALANCE		
General Government		
Personnel	$ 335,000.00	
Supplies	17,000.00	
Other Charges	131,000.00	
Capital Outlays	69,000.00	
Total General Government		$ 552,000.00
Public Safety		
Personnel	$ 528,000.00	
Supplies	33,000.00	
Other Charges	90,000.00	
Capital Outlays	77,000.00	
Total Public Safety		728,000.00
Fire Protection		
Personnel	$ 133,000.00	
Supplies	16,000.00	
Other Charges	64,000.00	
Capital Outlays	66,000.00	
Total Fire Protection		279,000.00
Recreation		
Personnel	$ 73,000.00	
Supplies	21,000.00	
Other Charges	33,000.00	
Capital Outlays	54,000.00	
Total Recreation		181,000.00
Total Estimated Expenditures		$1,740,000.00
Budgetary Fund Balance		20,000.00
Total Estimated Expenditures and Budgetary Fund Balance		$1,760,000.00

© 2020 Cengage®. May not be scanned, copied or duplicated, or posted to a publicly accessible website, in whole or in part.

City of Moserville

Adjusted Trial Balance

December 31, 20--

ACCOUNT TITLE	DEBIT	CREDIT
Cash	63,486.00	
Taxes Receivable—Current		
Allowance for Uncollectible Taxes—Current		
Taxes Receivable—Delinquent	34,189.00	
Allowance for Uncollectible Taxes—Delinquent		9,500.00
Interest Receivable	1,695.00	
Allowance for Uncollectible Interest		500.00
Inventory of Supplies	3,520.00	
Accounts Payable		14,985.00
Notes Payable		
Unreserved Fund Balance		26,150.00
Reserve for Encumbrances—Current Year		
Reserve for Encumbrances—Prior Year		5,250.00
Reserve for Inventory of Supplies		3,520.00
Property Tax Revenue		1,725,000.00
Interest Revenue		7,625.00
Other Revenue		26,480.00
Expenditure—Personnel, General Government	318,250.00	
Expenditure—Supplies, General Government	17,510.00	
Expenditure—Other Charges, General Government	127,070.00	
Expenditure—Capital Outlays, General Government	71,070.00	
Expenditure—Personnel, Public Safety	512,160.00	
Expenditure—Supplies, Public Safety	32,340.00	
Expenditure—Other Charges, Public Safety	91,800.00	
Expenditure—Capital Outlays, Public Safety	80,080.00	
Expenditure—Personnel, Fire Protection	133,000.00	
Expenditure—Supplies, Fire Protection	16,800.00	
Expenditure—Other Charges, Fire Protection	61,440.00	
Expenditure—Capital Outlays, Fire Protection	68,640.00	
Expenditure—Personnel, Recreation	69,350.00	
Expenditure—Supplies, Recreation	21,630.00	
Expenditure—Other Charges, Recreation	34,650.00	
Expenditure—Capital Outlays, Recreation	55,080.00	
Estimated Revenues	1,760,000.00	
Appropriations		1,740,000.00
Budgetary Fund Balance		20,000.00
Encumbrance—Capital Outlays, Public Safety	5,250.00	
Totals	3,579,010.00	3,579,010.00

© 2020 Cengage®. May not be scanned, copied or duplicated, or posted to a publicly accessible website, in whole or in part.

Name ______________________ Date ____________ Class ____________

24-M MASTERY PROBLEM (continued)

2.

	BUDGET	ACTUAL	VARIANCE—FAVORABLE (UNFAVORABLE)

© 2020 Cengage®. May not be scanned, copied or duplicated, or posted to a publicly accessible website, in whole or in part.

24-M MASTERY PROBLEM (continued)

3.

© 2020 Cengage®. May not be scanned, copied or duplicated, or posted to a publicly accessible website, in whole or in part.

Name ______________________ Date ____________ Class ____________

24-M MASTERY PROBLEM (continued)

4.

JOURNAL

PAGE 24

	DATE	ACCOUNT TITLE	DOC. NO.	POST. REF.	GENERAL DEBIT (1)	GENERAL CREDIT (2)	CASH DEBIT (3)	CASH CREDIT (4)	
1									1
2									2
3									3
4									4
5									5
6									6
7									7
8									8
9									9
10									10
11									11
12									12
13									13
14									14
15									15
16									16
17									17
18									18
19									19
20									20
21									21
22									22
23									23
24									24
25									25
26									26
27									27

© 2020 Cengage®. May not be scanned, copied or duplicated, or posted to a publicly accessible website, in whole or in part.

24-M MASTERY PROBLEM (concluded)

5.

© 2020 Cengage®. May not be scanned, copied or duplicated, or posted to a publicly accessible website, in whole or in part.

Name ______________________ Date ____________ Class ____________

24-C CHALLENGE PROBLEM (LO5), p. 717

Completing the end-of-period work for a governmental organization

1.

JOURNAL

PAGE 29

	DATE	ACCOUNT TITLE	DOC. NO.	POST. REF.	GENERAL DEBIT (1)	GENERAL CREDIT (2)	CASH DEBIT (3)	CASH CREDIT (4)	
1									1
2									2
3									3
4									4
5									5
6									6
7									7
8									8
9									9
10									10
11									11
12									12
13									13
14									14
15									15
16									16
17									17
18									18
19									19
20									20
21									21
22									22

© 2020 Cengage®. May not be scanned, copied or duplicated, or posted to a publicly accessible website, in whole or in part.

24-C CHALLENGE PROBLEM (concluded)

2.

© 2020 Cengage®. May not be scanned, copied or duplicated, or posted to a publicly accessible website, in whole or in part.